Cliff Parker has b
Number One Hu
worse, he's prepa
The author of sev
as several funnies,
column in *Angler's*
His hobbies are fishing, frog fancying and working towards sainthood; his ambition is to be locked in a pub with Brigitte Bardot!

Also in this series:

THE OFFICIAL IRISH JOKE BOOK
THE OFFICIAL IRISH JOKE BOOK NO 3 (BOOK 2 TO FOLLOW)
THE OFFICIAL SCOTTISH JOKE BOOK
THE WORLD'S WORST JOKE BOOK
THE OFFICIAL OZ JOKE BOOK
THE OFFICIAL IRISH JOKE BOOK NO. 4
POSITIVELY THE LAST IRISH JOKE BOOK
THE OFFICIAL CAT LOVERS/DOG LOVERS JOKE BOOK
THE OFFICIAL BOOK OF BAWDY BALLADS

Cliff Parker

The Official Angler's Joke Book

Illustrated by Graham Allen

Futura Publications Limited

A Futura Book

First published in Great Britain by
Futura Publications Limited in 1979

ISBN : 0 7088 1670 3

Made and printed in Great Britain by
Hunt Barnard Printing Ltd., Aylesbury, Bucks.

Futura Publications Limited,
110 Warner Road,
Camberwell, London SE5.

INTRODUCTION

When I started compiling this book, I asked Number One Son, 'What's the oldest fishing joke you know?'

'You, dad,' he said.

Very funny.

It is a fact, however, that fishing jokes have the longest pedigree of any, possibly even pre-dating Adam and Eve jokes.

There is a species of macaque monkey which lives in the mangrove swamps in South East Asia, and which lives by catching fish. Before man even appeared on Earth, it's a fair bet that Fred Macaque staggered home and said to his mate, 'Sorry, love. Nothing for supper again. But you should have seen the one . . .'

'Don't give me that,' Missis Macaque probably replied. 'You've been at the banana oil again.' And fetched him one with a coconut.

Stone Age man probably hopped back fishless to the cave one day and said, 'Sorry I'm late, darling. A Tyrannosaurus Rex bit my leg off.'

'Which one?'

'How should I know. They all look alike to me.'

'Come home with another story like that,' said his wife. 'And you won't have a leg to stand on.'

Izaak Walton has long been hailed as the father of Angling as We Know It. But he cribbed a lot of his stuff from other writers. Which points to the likelihood that Izaak was henpecked, used fishing as an excuse to get away from his wife, spent most of his time in Ye Olde English Boozer, and then had to think up something to justify it.

A very worrying aspect of angling jokes is the image they present of the angler: shiftless, incompetent, unprincipled, drunken and pathologically untruthful.

I should now like to put the record straight. We're not a bit like that, lads, are we?

Are we?

Please yourselves . . .

CLIFF PARKER

'It's the wife's birthday today,' said Jim. 'I bought her a beautiful river rod.'
'Hey, she must have been pleased with that,' said his mate.
'Not really,' said Jim. 'She was expecting a fur coat.'

'I caught a pike today. Twelve inches.'
'That's not big. I've had hundreds of pike of twelve inches.'
'Between the eyes?'

As the anglers left the bank after a closely-fought match, one of them called to the steward who had supervised the weigh-in, 'Hey, mate, here's a biscuit for your dog.'
'Dog?' said the steward. 'I've got no dog.'
'Oh,' said the angler. 'You still rely on the old white stick, do you?'

'Does your angling club boast a match fishing team?'
'It *has* one, yes. But I couldn't say we boast about it.'

The wife kept making me sandwiches straight from the freezer when I went out fishing. In the end I had to go to the doctor.
'What is it, doc?' I said. 'Ulcers?'
'No,' he said. 'Frostbite.'

Wandering along the bank at the match was a chap with a tray and a sign saying, 'HOT DOGS AT POPULAR PRICES'.
'Here,' said the angler. 'Hot dog, please.'
'Certainly, sir. That'll be a pound.'
'A quid for a hot dog! That sign says, "Popular Prices".'
'*I* like 'em . . .'

'Are you the famous Harley Street plastic surgeon?'
'Yes.'
'Well could you do something with the lid of my polythene bait tin?'

A daring young man from Khartoum
Went wading straight into his doom.
        A large crocodile
        Saw him fishing the Nile
And bit the Khart right off his Oum.

This chap went to the psychiatrist and said, 'Doctor, I've got two problems. First of all, I think I'm a brace and bit. Secondly, I think I'm a fisherman.'
The psychiatrist said, 'I'll listen to the brace and bit thing, though there's a chance it might bore me. The fisherman thing, I won't listen to: I *know* it will bore me.'

Mary caught a little pike,
Its teeth were white as snow.
Now she can't sit on her bike
Without going, 'Wa-ha-ho!'

Henpecked Cecil was copping it again from his wife. 'I've noticed that when you tell people about that big fish you caught on holiday, you vary the length and weight of it for every different person.'

'Yes, my love,' said Cecil. 'I never tell a bloke more than I think he'll believe.'

At the Division One National match, a set of very expensive carbon fibre rods were left leaning against a tree with a note pinned to them saying: 'These rods belong to the potential Match Angler of the Year, who is also a heavyweight boxer, a Seventh Dan in Judo, an expert in Karate and Kung Fu, and who will be back in five minutes.'

When the angler came back for his rods, they weren't there. In their place was a note which read: 'Your rods nicked by a 400 metre potential Olympic champion. Won't be back at all.'

I keep very cool when I lose a fish, but where I spit nothing ever grows again.

Angler: 'Excuse me, conductor. Does this bus stop at the river?'
Conductor: 'If it doesn't, mate, there'll be a hell of a splash.'

'Darling,' said the angler's wife, 'I really can't wait until Christmas to tell you what I've bought you. I'm giving you a lovely new standard lamp for the living room, a sheepskin rug for my side of the bed and a musical jewel box for the dressing table. Now I've told you, what are you going to get for me?'
'A fixed spool reel, a landing net and a box of floats.'

I wouldn't say the match steward couldn't see what was going on, but he was wearing specs over his contact lenses. Must be fair to him, though: he's never been the same since his guide dog was put down.

The angler on the charter boat was hanging over the side, green in the face and suffering dreadfully from seasickness.
'I feel so awful,' he said. 'What shall I do?'
'Just relax,' said the skipper. 'You'll soon find out.'

Confucius he say,
Angler who leave off winter drawers
Feel chilly around December.

Cedric landed a huge conger in the boat, and the first thing it did was to sink its teeth in the toe of his welly. His mates prised the conger loose, but the experience left Cedric really shaken, and he needed three or four large rums to get over it. After the trip, all the lads went into the pub, and Cedric bought drink after drink on the strength of his lucky escape.

On the way home, he was well plastered. He walked with one foot on the pavement and one in the gutter, and couldn't work out why he kept bobbing up and down.

'Flaming conger,' he muttered. 'It must have bitten deeper than I thought – both legs were the same length this morning . . .'

The angler rushed into a shop and said to the girl, 'Quick, love. I've got a match in ten minutes. Let's have a pair of wellies, size twelve.'

The girl assistant said, 'I don't think you quite understand, sir. This isn't a shoe shop: this is a boutique.'

'All right, all right,' said the angler. 'Give us a pair of them French wellies, then.'

EPITAPH FOR AN ANGLER·

Here lies O'Hara
From Liffeydownlug.
When his boat filled with water
He pulled out the plug.

Young Randy was in a tent by the waterside, night fishing. Not on his own – he was attempting to do what a lot of young night fishers are rumoured to do.

'Give us a kiss, love,' he said to his young lady companion.

'In a minute, love,' she said. 'It's so peaceful round here. So romantic. Just listen to those crickets.'

'Those aren't crickets,' he said. 'They're zippers.'

Henpecked Cecil went with the club for a day's outing. At lunchtime all the lads trooped into a riverside cafe, and were confronted by a big bad-tempered waitress who obviously wasn't keen on anglers.

'Yes?' she barked at Cecil.

'Cup of tea please, love.'

'And?'

'Egg and chips, love. If you wouldn't mind.'

'Anything to follow? Come on! I haven't got all day!'

'Just one thing, love,' said Cecil. 'I'm feeling homesick – nag me.'

'My wife broke my best fishing rod this morning,' said Henpecked Cecil.

'Don't worry,' said his mate. 'You can always buy another one.'

'Yes,' said Cecil, 'but that won't stop my head from throbbing.'

Two anglers were walking along the river bank. One of them stuttered.

'Her . . . her . . . hey . . . ' he said. 'Did yer . . . Did yer . . . Did yer ser . . . ser . . . see that brunette in the bikini ser . . . ser . . . sunbathing back there?'

'What brunette in a bikini?'

'Ter . . . ter . . . too late. You've mer . . . missed her.'

A little farther along he said, 'Her . . . her . . . hey . . . Did yer . . . did yer . . . did yer . . . ser . . . ser . . . see that redhead sunbathing topless back there?'

'What redhead sunbathing topless?'

'Ter . . .ter . . too late. You've mer . . . missed her.'

A little farther still: 'Her . . . her . . . hey . . . Did yer . . . did yer . . . did yer . . . ser . . . see that blonde sunbathing absolutely star . . . star . . . starkers back there?'

'What blonde sunbathing starkers?'

'Ter . . . ter . . . ter . . . too late. You've missed her. Her her . . . hey . . . did yer . . . ser . . . ser . . . see –

By now his mate was thoroughly fed up. 'Of course I did!' he snapped.

'Then wer . . . wer . . . why did you tread in it then?'

A greedy young angler from Brum
Felt a terrible pain in his tum.
He said, 'Damn and blasters!
'I've eaten me casters.
'I thought those last crisps tasted rum.'

Noah was a keen fisherman, but he couldn't do a lot during the flood. By the time he'd caught two fish, he'd run out of worms.

'The wife's run off with the lodger.'
'I'm sorry to hear that. I bet you're upset.'
'I am indeed. But I'll just have to go fishing without him.'

The angler went home to his wife looking very sad. 'Since I won that Matchman of the Year award,' he said, 'life's been hell for me down at the club. All the lads keep calling me Big Head. As far as I know, I'm still the same modest bloke I've always been. Tell me I've not got a big head, love.'
'Of course not, sweetheart,' said his wife. 'They're just jealous. Take no notice.'
'Thank you, pet,' said the angler. 'I feel better for that. I'm just popping out again for a couple of stones of loose groundbait. Have you got a big plastic bag I can carry it in?'
'I haven't, love,' said his wife. 'But don't worry — use your cap.'

Since the wife's been wearing mudpacks it's got very confusing. She had one on in bed the other night when I got home from fishing. I walked right round her: thought she was a swamp.

The old angler returned to the clubhouse to pick up some gear he had left in the store room. As he approached the door, he heard:
'Whose little smoochy-pie are you?'
'Your little smoochy-pie.'
'And whose little dimples are these?'
'My little dimples.'
'And whose little hands are these?'
'My little hands.'
'And whose little feet are these? And whose little toesie-poesies? And whose little feet . . . '
'When you get to the landing net,' shouted the old angler through the door, 'it's mine.'

'I was chilled to the bone when I went fishing this morning,' said Henpecked Cecil.
'Told you,' said Mrs Cecil. 'You should have put your hat on.'

Dopy Alec tripped over an abandoned rod on the bank. The rod had a reel and line attached, but no float or hook.
'Let's see now,' said Alec. 'I've either found a rod or lost a fish . . . '

EPITAPH FOR AN ANGLER:
Poor old Joe.
He didn't know
That when you dropped anchor
You had to let go.

The angler wanted his infant son to have all the fishing tackle he could never afford as a boy. So he went into a tackle shop and bought the lot – rods, reels, lines, nets, hooks, floats – all on tick and on very steep HP terms. He had to work overtime every week to keep up the payments, but finally cleared them all off. As he paid the last instalment, the tackle dealer said, 'That's it, then. Clean slate. By the way, how's the baby?'
'Fine,' said the angler. 'He gets married next week.'

Two mates were fishing on a windswept river bank. It had been raining in torrents all morning, it was bitterly cold, and they hadn't caught a thing. One of them turned to the other and said, 'Tell me again, Jim. I keep forgetting. We're not raving mad, are we, Jim? And we *are* having a good time, aren't we?'

Henpecked Cecil's wife was going on about him again. 'He's so lazy,' she said to Missis-Nextdoor, 'that the only reason he took me to Venice for our holiday was so he could fish from the bedroom window.'

'There I was, quietly fishing away,' said the angler, 'when this beautiful girl fell into the river and screamed for help. I dived in straight away, brought her back to the bank, and gave her artificial recreation.'
'You mean "respiration",' said his mate. 'I know all about life-saving methods. Recreation is when you're enjoying yourself.'
'You stick to your methods,' said the angler, 'and I'll stick to mine.'

Little boy sitting on the street corner, fishing in a bucket. Along comes the vicar, takes pity on the simple wee would, and gives him 10p.
'And how many have you caught today, little man?' he asks.
'You're the fourth,' says the little lad.

Drunken angler: 'I shay, where am I?'
Sober angler: 'You're at number 17 lock, just south of bridge 43, on the Grand Union Canal.'
Drunken angler: 'Never mind the details. Which county?'

Mate: 'Have you ever seen one of those machines that can tell when a bloke is lying?'
Henpecked Cecil: 'Seen one? I married one.'

Mary, jilted by a bailiff bold, said, 'Darling, give me a reason.'
Said he, 'Some time you've got to be told – You caught me out of season.'

The match fishing team came down from the North and won an important trophy against a London team. After the match, they had a wild night of celebration in the capital.
Harold met a young lady in Soho and they spent the night together in a hotel separate from the rest of the team. Next morning, having rung his original hotel room and had no reply, Harold's wife sent a telegram to every member of the team asking if they knew where he was.
She had thirty telegrams in reply, all saying: DON'T WORRY. HAROLD SPENT NIGHT WITH ME.

Poor Harold. That night of naughtiness cost him plenty. He and the young lady took a double room at the hotel, signing in as Mr and Mrs. The next morning after breakfast, the young lady slipped away and Harold went to Reception to pay the bill. It came to more than £100.
'Impossible!' said Harold. 'I've only been here one night.'
'*You* have, sir,' said the clerk. 'But your wife has stayed here a fortnight.'

'Can Sidney come out fishing, Mrs Jones?'
'No, he can't. He's in the bath.'
'Can his rod come out fishing, then?'

Henpecked Cecil got home very late and very much the worse for wear.
'What do you mean, coming home at this time?' demanded Mrs Cecil.
'It was like this, my love. I backed myself heavily in the match, but I didn't even make third place so I lost the lot.'
'And what kind of an excuse is that for coming home at four o'clock in the morning?'
'Well, you don't expect me to stop out all night with only a few bob in my pocket, do you?'

A fisherman loaded down with baskets, rods and all sorts of paraphernalia, was trying to get on a bus.
'You can't come on here with that lot,' said the conductor, and rang the bell.
As the bus pulled away the angler shouted, 'You know what you can do with your flaming bus, don't you?'
'Yes,' said the conductor. 'And if you could have done it with all that gear, I'd have let you on.'

Dopy Alec never had the luck. The only time he caught a mermaid, the top half was the fish.

Confucius he say,
Man who sit on rod rest
Quickly go up in world.

The fishing team had lost fifteen matches in a row.
'Say what you like about our lads,' said a disconsolate supporter as he left the river bank, 'at least they're good losers.'
'*Good?*' said his mate. 'They're bloody perfect.'

'Has anyone ever told you what a brilliant angler you are?'
'No.'
'Well where did you get the idea from?'

Henpecked Cecil's trouble started on the very day of his wedding. Halfway through the reception he disappeared. Eventually the new Mrs Cecil tracked him down to the river bank, where he was fishing happily away.
'And what do you think you're doing on our very first day of married bliss?' she screamed.
'Here we go,' said Cecil. 'Nag, nag, nag . . .'

SONGS FOR SWINGING ANGLERS:
When I Grow Too Old To Bream
Tiddler On The Roof
It Don't Mean A Thing If You Ain't Got That Ling

Henpecked Cecil was off for a weekend's trout fishing on his own.
'Did you pack the camping stove, my love?' he asked his wife. 'I'll be living off the land and frying what I catch.'
'Yes, I did,' said Mrs Cecil. 'But just to be on the safe side I've packed a tin of pilchards and a can opener.'

I'm getting fed up with the luncheon meat sandwiches the wife keeps giving me for my fishing trips. They taste lovely. But I've been mugged three times this week by barbel.

The team captain was giving the anglers the pep talk before the match.
'Remember what I've told you, lads,' he said. 'There's nothing like match fishing for building character, initiative, individuality, self-reliance and independence. Now get on that bank and do as you're told.'

The angler walked into the vet's surgery carrying an aquarium tank.
'My pet pike's just bitten my mother-in-law,' he said.
'What do you want me to do?' said the vet. 'Put it down?'
'No. Sharpen its teeth.'

A poorly-clad angler from Widnes
Caught a terrible cold in his kidneys.
His little short vest
Didn't cover his chest
And the long johns he wore were young Sidney's.

After the fishing match the captain hauled up Dopy Alec for a telling off.
'Look,' he said. 'I know you're new to match fishing. And I'm perfectly willing to accept that you only learned the knack this afternoon. But what I want to know is *what time* this afternoon?'

The vicar saw old Elijah and the village flirt coming out of the undergrowth by the river bank.
'Oh, yes,' he said, suspiciously. 'And what have you two been doing?'
'Fishing,' said Elijah. 'And when you get to my age, that's about all you *can* do.'

A motorist saw a sign outside a trout farm: '*Fresh trout for sale, £1.50 each.*'
He called in, bought a couple, then said to the trout farmer, 'You do raise these yourself, don't you?'
'Oh, yes,' said the farmer. 'Yesterday they were only £1 each.'

Jim was about to get married. In the pub with his father, he said, 'Dad, have you any advice before I take the Big Step?'
'Yes son,' said his father. 'Two things. One: insist on having one night a week out fishing with the lads.'
'Great, dad. And . . . ?'
'Two: don't waste it out fishing with the lads.'

'I'm not taking *her* fishing with me again,' said young Tommy, indicating his little sister with disgust. 'She spoiled the whole thing.'
'Why?' asked his mother. 'Did she make a lot of noise?'
'No. She ate all my worms.'

'It seems that your right arm – your casting arm, is it? – has seized up,' said the doctor, who fished for a rival team. 'But I shouldn't worry about it.'
'No,' said Albert. 'And if your flaming casting arm seizes up I won't cry over that, either.'

After a weekday's fishing with the vicar, Fred said, 'What do you think, Reverend: would it be a sin for me to fish on a Sunday?'
'The way you fish,' answered the vicar, 'it's a sin any day of the week.'

EPITAPH FOR AN ANGLER:
The reason Fred's
No longer here
Was a very long walk
On a very short pier.

The two worst fishermen in the world had been having bite after bite, but had not been able to hook a single fish.
'Getting boring, this,' said one. 'Tell you what – let's just miss two more fish and then go home.'

The scruffy, smelly angler walked into the doctor's surgery with a vague complaint. The doctor examined him and said, 'I'm not quite sure what's wrong with you, but this cannot fail to help. Take it three times a day with water.'
'What is it?' said the angler.
'Soap.'

The Martian reported back to his leader after a fact-finding mission on Earth.

'The Earthlings have a very strange custom, O Six-Headed One,' he said. 'They call it fishing.

'Lots of them work very hard so that they can buy strange wands and sharp hooks. They also buy great quantities of the foods they call bread, cheese, sausages, and also the larvae of a blue flying insect.

'Then they go down to the waterside and, in a mass ritual, throw much of this food upon the water. Some of it, also, they stick on the sharp hooks which are attached by lines to the wands.

'In this manner they capture quantities of water-dwelling creatures called fish, which according to my information are nourishing as food.'

'Interesting,' said the leader. 'And what do they do with these fish creatures?'

'When the ceremony is over,' said the Martian, 'they throw them all alive back into the water again.'

The 18 eyes in the Leader's six heads narrowed to slits and he quivered with rage.

'They told me!' he screamed. 'They told me before you set off for Earth and I should have listened. Next time I'll send somebody sober!'

'Look, daughter,' said the father of one of Randy's girl-friends. 'That youth with whom you've spent a lot of time night fishing is very far from being polished.'

'You're right, papa,' said the girl, blushing. 'He is a little rough around the hedges.'

'The staple industry of Iceland,' said the teacher, 'is fishing. In fact, in some parts of the country they use fish instead of money.'
'Bet it makes a hell of a mess of the fruit machines,' muttered little Tommy.

Bailiff: 'Does this rod belong to you?'
Angler: 'No. I've got three more instalments to pay on it.'

'I say! Why are you hitting that little boy?'
'We lost an important fishing match.'
'So?'
'He's our mascot.'

The tackle dealer was doing the hard sell.
'This handwarmer, sir,' he said, 'is ideal for the cold weather. It will burn for 12 hours without filling.'
'Is that so?' said the angler. 'And how long will it burn if you fill it?'

The steward at the fishing match had made himself very unpopular by disqualifying three of the home team for trifling technical offences. At the end of the match he came up to the home captain and said, 'Have you got a 2p piece for the phone? I want to call a friend.'
'Here are two 2p pieces,' said the captain. 'Call all your friends.'

What a great 'A' team we had last year. We fished against a team from Wigan and beat the pants off 'em. We fished against a team from Birmingham and beat the pants off 'em. We fished against a team from London and beat the pants off 'em. The match against an all-girls team was cancelled.

Mary said to the little shark,
'Come quietly or you'll cop it.'
The shark was feeling peckish that day,
Now Mary's got to hop it.

The angler turned up at the fly fishing school to try for a certificate in casting. It was obvious after his first few casts that he didn't know the first thing about it.
'How many lessons have you had?' asked the examiner.
'None.'
'I thought as much. Now don't waste my time. Come back when you've had a few.'
The angler went away and returned a few hours later, drunk as a lord.
'All ri',' he said, waving his rod wildly about. 'Ready when you are . . . '

The angler was hit on the head during a match by a large leger weight. He lay unconscious on the bank as his mates crowded round him.
'Give him some brandy and some air,' shouted someone.
The angler sat bolt upright. 'Just hurry up with the brandy,' he said. 'I can do without the air.'

He's a man who fishes religiously – every Sunday afternoon.

Offshore boat fishing is very character building. If there's anything in you, the sea will bring it out.

Henpecked Cecil had not had a nibble in a whole morning's fishing, so he stopped off at the fishmonger's on the way home.
He stood on the pavement outside and called to the fishmonger, 'Would you mind throwing me two of those trout from the slab, please?'
'Certainly. But why throw them?' said the fishmonger.
'So that I can look the wife straight in the eye,' said Cecil, 'and tell her I caught them.'

After the casting tournament, Dopy Alec went up to his team captain and said, 'OK. OK. I'm sorry. I accept that with somebody else in my place you would have won. I really fluffed those accuracy tests. All I want to do now is go home and shoot myself.'
'Not a bad idea,' said the captain. 'Make sure you've got a few spare rounds . . .'

A FISHERMAN'S PRAYER:
Lord, grant to me before I die
A fish so huge that even I,
When speaking of it afterwards,
Will never have the need to lie.

Confucius he say,
Knee-high water quite safe
Unless angler standing on head.

The angler got back from a sea trip and went into a fishmonger's.

'It's my wife's birthday and I've caught nothing to give her as a present,' he said. 'Have you got half a dozen mackerel?'

The girl assistant said, 'Have I got half a dozen mackerel? That doesn't sound very romantic.'

'Sorry,' said the angler. 'Sweetie Pie. Precious. Blue Eyes. Light of my Life. Have you got half a dozen mackerel, darling, please?'

'I don't like the look of that plaice you've caught,' said Henpecked Cecil's wife.

'If I'd known you wanted looks,' said Cecil, 'I'd have tried for goldfish.'

Two anglers had read that shark skin had commercial value, and decided to make their fishing trip pay for itself.
One of them was a gambler, and he bet his mate that he would catch the first shark and skin it. Sure enough, he caught the first shark – a monster – and hauled it on to the deck where it thrashed about and snapped its great jaws, biting huge chunks out of the mast.
'You be skinning that one, Joe,' said the angler. 'And I'll cast out for another.'

Henpecked Cecil turned up late for the match.
'What kept you?' said the steward.
'The wife wanted me to go with her to see her mother,' said Cecil. 'But she agreed in the end that I could toss up for it.'
'So? Tossing a coin doesn't take long.'
'It does when you have to do it 23 times.'

The angler on a charter boat was walking along the deck with a bowl of Russian salad. The boat pitched and the salad shot out of the bowl, all down the clean new anorak of a large, broken-nosed individual who had nodded off in a chair by his rod. Quick as a flash, the angler shook him and said, 'Better out than in, Squire. Are you feeling better now?'

The match angler was drowning his sorrows in the pub. 'Know what the captain had the nerve to say after today's match,' he said to his mate. 'He said, "Johnson, you're a disgrace to the team. A complete, utter and total disgrace". '
'Take no notice,' said his mate. 'You know what the captain's like. Always repeating what other people say.'

A keen angler is one who goes fishing when his television set isn't broken.

A keen salmon angler from Melton
Went wading without any belt on.
    His very first cast
    Left his pants at half mast,
And he soon had a well-mended kelt on.

The fishing team were gathering for the fray when the captain noticed that one of the lads was missing.
'Oh, I forgot,' said his mate. 'He did say something about getting married at two o'clock.'
'Blast!' said the captain. 'He'll have to get his skates on to make it here before the three o'clock whistle.'

Henpecked Cecil's wife was expecting company and she warned him not to tell any tall fishing stories to the guests.

Cecil restrained himself for an hour after their arrival, but when Mrs Cecil went into the kitchen he began, 'Yes. I got stuck into this pike. It must have been all of five feet long – '

Just then Mrs Cecil came out of the kitchen and fixed Cecil with a steely stare.

' – And just over half an inch wide . . . '

'Do you like buckling?'

'I don't know. I've never buckled.'

The steward had made himself very unpopular with both sides during the fishing match and had handed out some quite unjustified disqualifications.

'By heck,' whispered one of the competitors to his neighbour, 'he's going to be in hot water when this match is finished.'

'Just the opposite,' hissed his neighbour. 'He's going straight in the river.'

Telegram from Australia: SID KILLED BY SHARK.

Reply from wife: SEND HIM HOME.

Further telegram from wife: MISTAKE. ONLY SHARK IN COFFIN.

Reply from Australia: NO MISTAKE. SID IN SHARK.

The teacher was giving a lesson on Care of the Countryside.
'And why, children, should we never leave bottles on the river bank?'
'Because,' said a little lad on the back row, 'there might be money back on them.'

Two drunks were on a sea fishing trip. One held out his clenched fist and said, 'Guess what I'm holding in my hand?'
'A dogfish,' said the other one.
'Ah yes. But Lesser Spotted or Greater Spotted?'

EPITAPH FOR AN ANGLER:
Here lies Cecil.
He would have stayed longer.
But he tried to wrestle
With a bloody great conger.

ANGLING CLUB: A fountain of knowledge to which all go to drink.

The angler went into the pub, ordered a pint of bitter and a large scotch, drank the bitter and poured the scotch into his top pocket.

He repeated the order several times, and always did the same thing: drank the bitter, poured the scotch into his top pocket.

All the time, too, he was moaning. He grumbled about the locality, the facilities for fishing, the price of bait, the cost of day tickets, the scarcity of fish in what waters there were.

'All I've caught all week,' he said, 'is one miserable little gudgeon.'

He ordered another pint, another large scotch, and started yet another tirade.

'I'm not serving you,' said the landlord. 'You've had more than enough. And all you've done since you've come in here is moan. As if that's not bad enough you keep pouring large scotches into your top pocket. You're mad!'

'Listen,' said the angler. 'If you don't serve me, I'll jump over that bar, smash your teeth in and then beat you to a pulp!'

Just then a little gudgeon stuck its head out of the angler's top pocket.

'And that goes,' it said, 'hic! for your flaming cat as well . . .'

'Doctor, I've been knocking back a bottle of scotch every day for a fortnight to cure the rheumatism I got through fishing in this damp weather.'

'I can give you a prescription that will cure the rheumatism.'

'I don't want one. I came to see if I could get the scotch on the National Health.'

The angler walked into the club carrying a brand new, very expensive, carbon fibre rod.
'Nice one, that,' said Henpecked Cecil.
'Yes,' said the angler. 'I got it for the wife.'
'By heck,' said Cecil. 'I wish I could get a swop like that.'

The angler was late getting up for the first morning of his fishing holiday and he complained to the landlady of his digs that the alarm clock didn't go off at five o'clock as it was supposed to.
'Oh, dear, I forgot to tell you about that,' said the landlady. 'Sometimes it seizes up and doesn't ring. If you hear it seizing up before it goes off, give it a shake and it'll ring. If it still doesn't ring, leave it till about ten past five and give it another shake.'

Mary hooked a little whale.
It filled her full of cheer.
But the last words heard on board the boat
Were, ' 'S'awful dark in here . . . '

When young Randy took up night fishing, he didn't do it just for the fish. Nor did he believe in wasting time. When he lured the young lady into his tent he said, 'I'm a man of few words, darlin'. Do yer or don't yer?'
The young lady simpered. 'You talked me into it. You silver-tongued devil, you . . . '

The tourists were being shown round an Irish castle by an old retainer. They came eventually to a gigantic pike skull mounted on the wall.

'That thing there,' said the guide, 'is the skull of the Giant Pike of Ballymuckduffin, which used to swallow whole cows alive. Took six horses and twelve men to drag it from the water, so it did. And that pike, yer honours, was a hundred years old. Just think of that: one hundred years old!'

One of the visitors pointed to a much smaller pike skull mounted nearby.

'And what's that?' he asked.

'That, yer honour,' said the guide, 'that is the skull of the same pike when it was only twenty five.'

The angler looked along the bank and there, fishing a few yards away, was a frog.

'Don't see many frogs fishing along this bank,' he said, by way of conversation.

'Not surprised,' said the frog. 'Until just before you came along I was a feller.'

'Is that so? And when did you turn into a frog?'

'Just after I told that old gypsy lady what to do with her lucky white heather.'

A riot broke out at the weigh-in of a needle match. One of the anglers, a six-foot-six giant, picked up a little fellow from the opposition and swung him high above his head.

'Hey up, don't waste him!' yelled a supporter. 'Throw him at the steward!'

The small boy fell into the river. Immediately an angler dived in after him, caught up in the fast water just before the weir, and struggled back with him to the bank. Through the congratulatory crowd a burly man pushed his way.

'You the bloke who rescued my boy?' he asked.

'Yes,' said the angler, blushing modestly.

'Well, what's happened to his cap?'

'What sort of team do you think you'll have for the match on Saturday?'

'The usual. Six anglers, nine phone calls and three telegrams.'

Confucius he say,
Hook in fish
Worth two in finger.

A little boy fishing was grabbed by the bailiff.

'Can't you see that notice?' he roared.

'Oh, yes,' said the lad. 'But it said PRIVATE at the top, so I didn't read any further.'

The old match angler was past his best and he had been kept in the team more out of sympathy than anything else. But after an end-of-season losing run of six matches, a new and ruthless team captain was appointed.

The first thing the new captain did was to call in the old boy.

'I assume you want to know if I can fish for the team next season,' beamed the veteran.

'Not on your life,' said the captain. 'I've never seen an angler like you. Your tackle's thirty years out of date. You can't see a float beyond five yards. You can't even see to the swingtip on the end of your rod, come to that. You can't bait up with a maggot without sticking the hook in your finger. You can't cast without hooking somebody behind you. You're so slow on the strike that the fish has time to call in a second opinion. You can't play a fish bigger than a stickleback without losing it. You make such a splash with your landing net that every fish within a hundred yards disappears. You're so hopeless that I wouldn't even trust you to sell popcorn on the bank. I never want to see your stupid face at my matches again! Now get out!'

'Ah,' said the old boy. 'Am I to take it, then, that you'd like time to think it over?'

Jim: 'Hello, Alec. I see you're wearing your long underpants. Very sensible for fishing in this weather.'

Dopy Alec: 'Yes, I am. But how did you know?'

Jim: 'You've forgotten to put your trousers on.'

The angler had been taking a little something to keep out the cold, and by the time he packed up he was definitely the worse for wear. He loaded his gear into the car and started off.

'Floods,' he thought, as water began to slosh around his ankles. 'I didn't know we'd had any rain today. I'd better get back to the hotel quickly.'

He wound down the window and called to a passing farmer, 'Which is the quickest way to town?'

'By road, I reckon,' said the farmer. 'Takes a lot longer by river.'

'How did your team do in the match this afternoon?'

'We won: Seven to two.'

'What do you mean, seven to two? Fish? Pounds? Ounces?'

'Black eyes.'

A night fishing addict from Settle
Was feeling on top of his mettle.
        To his tent dark and shady
        He took a young lady
And now he's in no kind of fettle.

The stewards on a big fishing match were over-zealous and disqualified several anglers for trifling infringements of the rules. One angler was disqualified merely for asking his mate at the next peg how he was getting on.
After the match he walked across the bridge over the river, singing, 'Twenty one today . . . Twenty one today . . . ' and stretching his arms out at full length as if to demonstrate the size of a giant fish.
The steward who disqualified him strode up and said, 'Don't be so damned silly. You didn't catch a thing in that match and now you're walking around holding your arms out singing, "Twenty one today". If there's one thing worse than a lousy fisherman, it's a liar. Would you mind explaining yourself?'
The angler picked up the steward and threw him over the bridge into the river.
Then he walked on, arms outstretched, singing, 'Twenty two today . . . Twenty two today . . . '

Anglers are renowned as a race of long livers.
Some of them have livers three feet long.

The conservationist giving a talk to the angling club said, 'Let's really be honest with ourselves, gentlemen. How many of us here tonight have actually done anything to conserve our fish stocks?'
'On yer feet, lads!' shouted the match team captain.

Angler to young lady holidaymaker: 'Sorry, miss, but you're not allowed to swim in this stretch of river. It's against the law.'
Young lady: 'Why didn't you tell me that when you saw me undressing?'
Angler: 'There's no law against undressing.'

The angler caught a massive catfish which almost certainly broke the record by tens of pounds. He had no scales with him, so he dumped the fish in an old pram and started pushing it to the local Report Station.
He was stopped on the way by a shortsighted old lady who looked into the pram, gazed down at the slimy, big-mouthed, bewhiskered fish and said, 'My, my – isn't he like his father?'

The angler lurched up the bank to a fellow piscator.
'Hey,' he said. 'Do you drink?'
'Of course not,' said the other.
'Good. Hold this bottle while I tackle up.'

The weigh-in at the fishing match was in full swing when Henpecked Cecil pushed his way through the throng from the back.
'Would you mind checking my catch now?' he said.
'Only I've just heard that the wife's been taken seriously ill.'

The angler staggered up to the match venue in a hell of a state: bruised, battered, scarred, streaming with blood, clothes in shreds and hardly able to limp up to his peg.
'Where the hell have you been?' demanded the team captain. 'You're supposed to check in at least an hour before the whistle.'
'Sorry,' gasped the angler. 'I fell out of a seven-storey window.'
'Oh yes,' said the captain. 'And it took you an hour?'

In his excitement at hooking a big fish, the angler fell off the end of the pier.
'Help,' he screamed. 'I can't swim! I can't swim!'
A drunk stuck his head over the rail. 'So what?' he said. 'I can't play the violin, but I don't go round shouting about it.'

'What's Dopy Alec fishing for today?'
'Practice, I reckon.'

EPITAPH FOR AN ANGLER:
Fred went underwater fishing,
Now he's no longer laffin'.
Someone mistook him for a skate
And put a damn great gaff in.

'Our team may not have won,' said the match angler. 'But the weights we caught this afternoon didn't really do us justice.'
'You're team doesn't want justice,' said his mate. 'It wants mercy.'

Two mates used to go fishing together every week. One invariably caught more than the other. Sometimes he fished the opposite bank of the river. And sometimes he failed to turn up at all.
One day his mate said, 'How come you always catch more than me, sometimes fish from the opposite bank and sometimes just don't turn up at all?'
'It all depends on the wife,' said his mate. 'If she's lying on her left side when I wake up in the morning, I fish the left bank of the river. If she's lying on her right side, I fish the right bank.'
'What if she's lying on her back?'
'Those are the days I don't turn up at all.'

'Would you rather a shark ate you or a piranha?'
'I'd rather the shark ate the piranha.'

'I went fishing with my wife yesterday,' said the club bore.
'Lucky you,' said Henpecked Cecil. 'I'm still using worms.'

The angler landed a monster pike and made the mistake of turning his back on it as it lay on the bank. It gave a mighty leap and sank its teeth in the angler's rear.
As he was having it treated at the local infirmary he said, 'Well, I suppose that's what comes of trying to break a record.'
'You broke a record, all right,' said the doctor.
'You're the first man round here to climb down a tree without climbing up it first.'

Bailiff: 'I've caught you poaching. Name please?'
French angler: '*Je ne comprends pas.*'
Bailiff: 'How do you spell it?'

A home team supporter at a fishing match, lurching towards the bank, was stopped by a steward.
'Just a minute,' said the steward. 'I don't think you'd better go any further. You're drunk.'
'Of course I'm drunk,' said the fan. 'You don't think I'd come and watch this lot sober, do you?'

'Caught anything yet?'
'Not unless you count double pneumonia.'

'Catch much?' asked the barman.

'A hundred or two,' said the angler.

'A hundred or two? Never. I'll bet you a fiver you didn't.'

'Done.'

'Right. There's the fiver. Where's your catch?'

The angler put two fish on the bar and picked up the money.

'Told you I'd caught a hundred or two. And it definitely wasn't the hundred.'

The club went on an outing to the seaside and fished all day from a rickety old jetty.

In the evening, everybody packed up and returned to the coach park except Dopy Alec. After half an hour the coach driver said, 'I can't wait much longer for Alec. One of you had better fetch him.'

Alec's mate went back to the jetty and, sure enough, Alec was still standing there.

'Getting dark, Alec.'

'Yes, it is.'

'Time to go home.'

'I know.'

'The coach driver won't wait much longer.'

'I thought he wouldn't.'

'Well, are you coming.'

'No, I'm not.'

'Why not?'

'I can't.'

'Why can't you?'

'I've got my foot stuck between the boards.'

4

Mary caught a little ling,
It looked a lot like pollack,
But as it took her finger off,
She knew she'd dropped a clanger.

The angler gave a massive backswing to his cast and the heavy leger weight struck a cow right between the eyes and killed it stone dead.
Confronted by the angry farmer, the angler said, 'I'm sorry. Entirely my fault, I've killed your cow. Can I replace her?'
'Depends,' said the farmer. 'How many gallons a day do you give?'

'You're out of the club team,' said the captain. 'Out. Through. Finished.'
'Oh, yes,' said the disgruntled angler. 'And who do you propose to get to fill the gap?'
'Gap?' said the captain. 'I wasn't aware that you'd be leaving one.'

'If you wanted to go fishing,' said Henpecked Cecil's wife, 'why didn't you ask me first?'
'Because,' said poor old Cecil, 'I wanted to go.'

'How do you normally fish a match?'
'With a false beard, ginger wig and under an assumed name.'

The gods gave man Eve, and he took to eating apples. They gave him marriage and he took up fishing.

Lost in a storm, the angler called at a lonely old farm and asked whether he could be put up for the night.
'Certainly,' said the farmer. 'But you'll have to sleep with my son.'
'Hell,' said the angler. 'I'm in the wrong joke.'

To be fair, the farmer did find the angler a place downstairs on the settee. In the early hours of the morning, the farmer came to check that he was comfortable.
'Be a very cold noight, this be,' he said, falling into the accent demanded of farmers in commercial traveller jokes. 'Would 'ee loike our eiderdown?'
'Thank you very much,' said the angler. 'But she's been down twice already.'

'Don't despair,' said the bailiff to the luckless angler. 'There are plenty of good fish left in this swim.'
'I know,' said the angler. 'I'm the bloke who left them there.'

The old angler suffered from constipation through sitting so long on the bank.
The doctor advised castor oil. So the angler bought a gallon of it and drank it before he went fishing.
Though he was dead on arrival at hospital, everyone along the river reckoned he'd had a good run for his money.

One day Henpecked Cecil rebelled.
'I'm homesick!' he cried.
'But this is your home,' said Mrs Cecil.
'I know! And I'm sick of it!'

Anglers' wives are to blame for a lot of the lying their husbands do. They will ask questions.

'Tommy,' said the teacher, 'do you know how fast carp grow?'
'Yes, Miss. An inch a day.'
'How do you work that out?'
'My dad caught a carp a fortnight ago, and to hear him talk it's grown at least a foot since then.'

Notice in an Irish country lane: When you can't see this sign, the river is under water.

A ginger-haired angler from Eccles
Broke out into terrible freckles.
        They spread from his tum
        Right round to his bum
And up to the back of his neckles.

At the parish council meeting, the question of improving a local stretch of water was raised. Some councillors wanted to develop it for boating, others for angling.
Councillor Jones stood up and said, 'I would suggest turning it into an ornamental lake and buying a gondola.'
'False economy!' shouted one of the fishing lobby. 'Why don't we buy a pair of gondolas and let 'em breed?'

The angler was out. Back home, his wife was in bed with his best friend.
The bedside phone rang, and the wife answered it. 'That was Fred,' she said to the best friend. 'He's out fishing with you.'

Heard about the angler who lost his cap in a field of cows?
He tried on fifty before he found his own.

'Is this river any good for fish?'
'It must be bloody marvellous – I can't get any of them to leave it.'

Magistrate: 'What made you think the defendant was drunk?'
Policeman: 'Firstly, your worship, he was fishing in the fountains in Trafalgar Square. Secondly, he was pointing to the lions and shouting up to Nelson, "Hey, mate – those flaming things should be on a lead on the towpath!" '

Fred was proud of the number of fish he'd caught, but he was pretending to be modest.
'Just lucky, I suppose,' he said to his mate. 'I must have run into a school.'
His mate lifted up Fred's keepnet and squinted inside.
'You ran into a school all right,' he said. 'And you've made a right mess of the infants' class.'

Bailiff: 'What's your name?'
Poacher: 'John Smith.'
Bailiff: 'Pull the other one. You're the fifth John Smith today. What's your real name?'
Poacher: 'Johann Sebastian Bach.'
Bailiff: 'Thanks Taffy. That's more like it.'

EPITAPH FOR AN ANGLER:
Here lies Joe
Who fished for the larder.
He had to go
When a shark pulled harder.

'I've just come back from a fishing holiday in the Lake District. Lovely run from the hotel to the water: only two straight roads and a flyover junction.'
'Marvellous. Where did you stay?'
'The Hilton Hotel in London.'
'But that's more than 250 miles from the Lakes. What were the roads?'
'The M1 and the M6.'

The two Irish lads had caught dozens and dozens of big fish from a rowing boat.
'We'll have to come back to this spot tomorrow, Liam,' said one of them.
'Sure, but how will we find it?'
'Simple. I'll put a chalk mark on the side of the boat.'
'Dont be daft, Mick. We may not get the same boat tomorrow.'
'Of course we will. I'll make sure of that. And I'll ask the feller at the boatyard to keep an eye on the chalk mark in case anyone tries to rub it off.'

The angler was fishing a lake deep in the heart of a safari park when a hippo emerged from the water, smashed his rods and trampled all over his gear.

The angler left his tackle and staggered back to his car, to find a troop of monkeys pulling off his windscreen wipers. He chased them away, got in the car, and had just moved off when a kangaroo leapt out of the undergrowth and crashed into the aerial, bending it very badly. By this time he was in a foul temper, so when an elephant crossed the track in front of him, he screeched up to it, slammed on his brakes and hooted loudly.

The elephant looked around calmly, kicked in the rear wing, then sat on the bonnet and caved it in.

The angler roared off to the park warden's hut and hammered on the door.

'Look at the mess your animals have made of my car!' he yelled when the warden answered the door. 'I demand compensation!'

'Oh, my dear sir,' said the warden. 'Do come in. How can I apologise? Here, drink this scotch for your nerves.'

Down went the scotch in one and the warden poured out another tumblerful.

The angler was calming down by now, and he and the warden had quite a long chat about the hazards of the park. Every five minutes the warden filled up the tumbler, and before long the whole bottle of whisky had disappeared.

The angler was halfway home, his car weaving all over the road, when he was pulled up by a police patrol car.

'Been in the wars by the looks of things, sir,' said the officer. 'Like to tell me how it happened?'

'Yish,' said the angler. 'Windshcreen wipers . . . bunch of monkeys pinched 'em. Aerial . . . flaming kangaroo bent it. Damn great elephrump kicked the side in then sat on the bonnet . . . ' (*Continued p.58*)

'Of course, sir,' said the officer. 'And do you mind telling me where you've been?'
'Fishing, of course,' said the angler. 'What does it look like?'
'Where is your tackle, sir?'
'Smashed to smithereens. A bloody great huppo . . . hitto . . . hittotopamus jumped all over it.'
'Silly me,' said the officer. 'I should have realized. Could you do just one more small thing for me, sir?'
'Shertainly,' said the angler. 'What is it?'
'Just blow into this little bag . . .'

She was only an angler's daughter
But she wouldn't swallow any old line.

'My dad's got more than a hundred medals for fishing.'
'What is he, an ace matchman?'
'No. He's a pawnbroker.'

Mary to her boyfriend said,
'Tell me what you're wishing?'
'Having just met your mama, my love,
'I'm wishing I'd gone fishing.'

An angler fishing the canal near the local lunatic asylum noticed another angler, obviously let out for the day, walking along the bank and sprinkling powder into the water.
'What are you doing that for?' he asked.
'Shark repellent, this,' said the loony. 'Keeps the man-eating sharks away.'
'But there aren't any man-eating sharks in the canal.'
'I know. Bloody good powder, isn't it?'

The American on a sea fishing trip in the English Channel, just wouldn't stop boasting to the Englishman next to him.
'Out in the States,' he said, 'we don't stand any nonsense with infringements of the law. No, sir. We shoot first and ask questions afterwards. Why, I remember . . . '
Farther out in the Channel lay a drifting wreck, laden with high explosives, which the R.A.F. were blowing up as a danger to shipping. A squadron of jet planes roared overhead and plastered the wreck with bombs and rockets. The ship exploded with a thunderous roar, sending great sheets of flame and clouds of smoke into the air and showering the surrounding water with debris.
'My God!' exclaimed the American. 'What the hell was that?'
'Dear me,' said the Englishman. 'I forgot to tell him.'
He went to the side of the boat, cupped his hands and shouted, 'Come in Number Seven, your time's up!'

The little boy came rushing up to his father on the river bank.
'Quick, dad, quick!' he cried. 'I want a lifebelt! Must have a lifebelt!'
'Shush,' said his father. 'I'm trying to fish, if you don't mind. Besides which, I don't happen to have a lifebelt.'
'Please yourself,' said the little boy. 'I'll just let mummy drown.'

The old angler kept getting disqualified in matches for not hearing the whistle for the finish. So he got one of the new transistorized hearing aids.
'Marvellous, this, Walter,' he said to one of his mates on the bank. 'So small you don't know you're wearing it.'
'Very pleased to hear it,' said Walter. 'Does it work?'
'Half past four,' said the angler.
'No, I mean can you hear better with it?'
'Much better now, thanks. Since she had the gallstones done, she's never looked back.'

'Athletics Anonymous' is doing a great job. If ever you get the urge to do something strenuous, like playing football, rugby or digging the garden, you just ring them. They send somebody over to take you fishing until the feeling wears off.

SHANTY FOR SEAFARING ANGLERS:
We jolly fishermen
Are up and up aloft
And our breakfasts are lying down below, below, below
And our breakfasts are lying down below . . .

Fred volunteered to put the anchor over the side of the charter boat, but he forgot to let go. Down to the bottom he went, but he pushed with all his might and swam back to the surface. His mates were waving and shouting to him, but before he could make any sense of it all, down he went again.
In all, he went down and back up again three times. By then he'd had enough. As he surfaced for the third time he shouted to his mates, 'Look! If one of you doesn't throw me a lifebelt soon, I'm going to let this flaming anchor drop!'

The angling club went on a mystery tour, starting from the clubhouse. And guess where the anglers were all taken? Home.

Two Irish lads were out fishing from a boat when the sails blew away.
'Don't worry, Seamus,' said the first one. 'We can use the engine.'
'The divvil we can,' said Seamus. 'We haven't a rope strong enough to tie it to the mast.'

Two roughneck anglers met in the pub on Saturday night.
'Good match this afternoon?' asked one.
'Yer,' said his mate. 'Argument at the weigh-in. Dozen punch-ups. Twenty arrests. Six coppers hurt and three stewards had their legs broken.
Best match for weeks.'

The angler was late for the charter boat. As he arrived on the quayside, the boat was moving off, so he took a flying leap, tackle and all. He landed on his head on the deck and knocked himself out. By the time he recovered consciousness, the boat was a quarter of a mile from land. He looked at the distant shoreline and said, 'By gum. A hell of a jump that was!'

Two muggers attacked Dopy Alec as he was leaving the canal towpath. After a hell of a fight, all they found in his pockets were a bit of sausage, a piece of luncheon meat and a paper bag with some squashed maggots in. 'Why the hell did you fight like that for a load of rubbish like this?' they asked.
'How was I to know?' said Alec. 'I thought you were after the fiver in my sock.'

'Cecil, why did you take your wife fishing the other day?'
'It was either that or kiss her goodbye.'

Confucius he say,
Fingers last longer
If kept out of conger.

Dopy Alec was sitting outside his house after a cloudburst, fishing in a puddle.
'That's a waste of time,' said a passing angler.
'There'll be no fish in there.'
'I know that,' said Alec. 'But it's not half as far to walk.'

The short-sighted match angler had been threatened with being dropped from the team if he didn't do something about his eyesight. So he went to the optician and got fixed up with a new pair of spectacles.
At the next match he fished, his peg was next to a telegraph pole.
'Right,' he said, peering round. 'I'm not sure whether the feller next door's rod is legal or not, but let's get cracking.'

'Didn't your wife mind your staying out all weekend fishing, Cecil?'
'Not a bit. I was going to have my front teeth out, anyway.'

Dopy Alec: 'Am I getting the hang of it now? Better than last week?'
Bailiff: 'Well, you're not catching any more. But at least you're not scaring so many.'

'My, you're doing well catching all those fish. What are you using?'
'Chewing tobacco and this brick.'
'How do you mean?'
'I put the chewing tobacco on the hook. Then when the fish come to the surface, I hit 'em with this brick.'

A chap who lived by the river went into the police station and banged a dead pike down on the counter. 'Somebody threw this in my front garden,' he said. 'What are you going to do about it?'
'Leave it with me,' said the desk sergeant. 'And if nobody's claimed it in six months, it's yours.'

The little boy was poaching on the river.
'Got you!' said the bailiff. 'And I've had enough of this. I'm taking you home to tell your father.'
'No need,' said the little boy. 'Tell him now – he's fishing just round the next bend.'

'My dad once caught a man-eating shark and he didn't turn a hair.'
'I'm not surprised – your dad's as bald as a coot.'

The poor old kipper went deaf, so his mates clubbed together to buy him a herring aid.

'How are things?'
'Could be better. The wife's run off with the lodger. The house has burned down. I've been barred from the pub and expelled from the angling club. Not only that, I've been disqualified from fishing matches for life for cheating. Oh, and I've lost my job.'
'Dear me. So how are you making a living?'
'Selling lucky charms on the bank.'

'None of my business,' said the nosy neighbour, 'but have you noticed what your daughter's been doing lately?'
'No,' said the mother. 'What?'
'Knitting little bootees and matinee coats.'
'Thank goodness for that. It makes such a change from going fishing with the boys.'

'But sweetheart,' said Henpecked Cecil. 'Why won't you believe I've been fishing?'
'Because,' said Mrs Cecil, 'when you came home you kissed the cat, gave me a saucer of milk, threw two kippers in the frying pan and shouted, "Those two were swimming free only an hour ago!" '

5

An Indian angler from Ootra
Was reciting some uplifting sutra
When a shark on the rise
Brought the tears to his eyes,
Now his Brahma's gone right down the Putra.

The specimen hunter's wife gave birth to a bouncing baby girl. The birth was at home and the midwife had forgotten her scales.

'Weigh her on mine,' said the proud father. 'I've weighed all my best catches on these.'

The baby girl made medical history when she weighed in at 34 pounds.

A night fisherman asked the doctor how he could improve his eyesight. The doctor told him to eat plenty of carrots with every meal. The angler was back a few weeks later, covered in scars, to complain about the diet.

'Can't you see any better?' asked the doctor.

'Oh, yes, but look at me. Bitten all over. Flaming carrots. I was out by the river last night and a fox chased me for a quarter of a mile along the bank.'

'Weren't you able to outrun it?'

'For a little way, yes. Then I tripped over my ears . . .'

Steward: What a match angler becomes when his eyesight starts to fail.

The angler had been sitting there all morning, fly-fishing for trout, and had not caught a thing.
Along came a man walking his dog and said, 'Trout, boy! Go fetch!'
The dog ran across the top of the water and came back with a big juicy trout in its jaws.
'Marvellous,' said the angler. 'I've been trying all morning. That's a really clever dog you've got there.'
'He'd be a damn sight cleverer,' said the dog owner, 'if he could swim.'

'Cecil! I've just about had enough of you smoking in bed.'
'But lots of people smoke in bed.'
'Kippers?'

Basso profundo: A deep-thinking fish.

An angler who had been bass fishing in the surf in his bare feet on a cold day came shivering up to the tea stall on the sands. He ordered a bucketful of tea.
'Surely you're not going to drink it out of the bucket?' said the stallholder.
'Drink it? I'm going to soak my feet in it.'

A clumsy angler on the pier cast out with a 4oz. lead. On the backswing it caught a holidaymaker right in the middle of the forehead and killed him stone dead. 'Never mind, love,' said the angler to the holidaymaker's grief-stricken wife. 'At least it missed his eye.'

The Supporters' Club bought each member of the fishing team a cigarette lighter for Christmas. Thought they may as well, as the anglers spent all season losing their matches.

Dopy Alec was always an asset to his angling club team. With his head they were always sure of at least one point.

The angler was fishing in a strange town in Ireland. He got on a bus and asked another passenger if he would tell him where to get off for the river.
'Certainly,' the man said. 'Just keep your eye on me and get off one stop before I do.'

Confucius he say,
Dibbling your dropper
Hard to explain to copper.

Two mates were fishing. One said to the other, 'Ooh, I'm dying for a jimmy riddle but there's no cover on this bank. And with all these couples taking their afternoon strolls I just daren't risk it.'
'No problem,' said his mate. 'Just wander up to that feller fishing farther along the bank and chat him up about his catch. While he's telling you all about it, you can do it in his pocket. It's waterproof.'
'No, I couldn't do that. He'd feel it.'
'No he wouldn't. You've not felt a thing yet, and I did it in yours ten minutes ago.'

'How can you tell when the shark are on the feed?'
'Dabble your feet in the water. If they come up with some toes missing, the shark are on the feed.'

The angler went to see the psychiatrist.
He said, 'Doctor, I keep having the most awful nightmare. I dream I fall overboard from this boat, and swimming towards me is the mother-in-law with a great big sea monster accompanying her.
'All the time they're getting closer and closer. I can see the huge, staring, bloodshot eyes . . . hear the horrible snorting noises . . . smell the foul, rancid breath . . . hear the gnashing of the huge, decaying, green teeth . . . '
'You poor chap,' said the psychiatrist. 'That really sounds horrible.'
'Yes,' said the angler. 'And just you wait till I tell you about the monster . . . '

'Look,' said the angler to his mate, 'I'll make all the arrangements for the day's fishing: buy the tickets, buy the bait, organize the tackle. You just get something for us to eat and drink. See you by the bridge in an hour.'
The mate turned up in an hour carrying six bottles of scotch and a loaf.
'You fool!' screamed the angler. 'Can't I leave anything to you? What are we going to do with all that bread?'

The explorer was telling of his adventures among the perils of the Amazon Basin.
'What about the piranha fish?' asked an angler in the audience. 'Are they as vicious as they're made out to be?'
'Not at all,' said the explorer. 'Tame as anything. Why, they'd eat off your hand.'

'Dad, do you know that old fishing rod that's been handed down in the family from generation to generation?'
'Yes.'
'Well this generation's just broken it.'

A sea angler out of Torquay
Felt a terrible pain in his knee.
He said, 'It's a conger!
'I've never seen longer.
'I hope it's not stopping for tea.'

The burly, broken-nosed angler went into the grocer's shop and asked for half a loaf of bread.
'I'm sorry, sir,' said the grocer. 'We don't sell half loaves. Why not a full one?'
'It's for bread paste,' said the angler. 'I don't need a full one. Now get me half a loaf before I do something drastic such as knotting your neck.'
'Just a minute, sir,' said the grocer, and went into the room at the back of the shop.
'There's a great, ugly, smelly lunatic out there,' he said to his wife, 'who wants half a loaf of bread.'
Then he noticed that the angler had followed him in.
'And this gentleman here wants the other half.'

'Who's that at the door?'
'A fisherman.'
'Tell him to sling his hook.'

'Johnny,' said mum, 'don't be so mean. Let your little sister play with your jar of tiddlers if she wants to.'
'No, mum, no! She wants to keep them!'
'What makes you think that?'
'She's swallowed three already!'

'And where do you think you've been till this time of night?' demanded Henpecked Cecil's wife.
'Ah . . . Well it was like this, my love. I was sitting on the canal bank minding my own business, when this flying saucer landed, and out got these little green men.
'They wanted to know about life on Earth, so I introduced them to some of the lads, took them for a pint, went for a ride on a bus . . . that sort of thing.
'They were keen to know about our system of government, so I took them on the train to London and we had tea with the Prime Minister at the House of Commons. I knew I mustn't be late back, so I left them chatting and caught the train back.
'I called at the canal to pick up my tackle and thought I'd have just one more try. So I cast out and got this beautiful perch, first go. Then I thought – '
'Just a minute,' said Mrs Cecil. 'Are you trying to tell me you caught a fish?'
'Yes, my love.'
'Now,' said Mrs Cecil, fetching him one with the frying pan, 'now I *know* you're lying!'

'What a dream I had last night,' said the angler to his mate. 'I was fishing on this beautiful river, fringed with palm trees and filled with the breeze-borne scents of a million tropical flowers. And who should come walking along the bank but Raquel Welch, Sophia Loren, Brigitte Bardot, Jane Fonda – all lusting after little old me. And there was no denying them: I had to let them all have their way with me . . . '
'It's nice to hear of a dream with a happy ending,' said the mate.
'I was just coming to that,' said the angler. 'Then I got stuck into this 50 lb. carp . . . '

Joe went into the bait shop and ordered a pint of maggots.
'Shall I wrap them up for you?' asked the proprietor.
'No,' said Joe. 'Just chuck 'em on the floor. I'll herd 'em home.'

EPITAPH FOR AN ANGLER:
There wasn't much of Harry
When we laid him on the deck.
A shark had bitten his big toe off,
Right up to the neck.

Two old chaps were fishing when a funeral cortege crossed the bridge over the canal. One laid down his rod, stood up, took his cap off and bowed his head.
'Ee, Albert, I didn't know you were sentimental,' said his mate. 'Or did you know the deceased?'
'I did,' said Albert. 'And she was always a good wife to me.'

Offshore boat fishing is certainly character building. If there's anything in you the sea will bring it out.

Bailiff: 'Do you know who I am?'
Drunken angler: 'No, mate, but just tell me your address and I'll see you get home all right.'

An Oxford angling club challenged one of the university fishing societies to a match.
On the morning of the game the match secretary sent the university lads a telegram saying: 'MAY THE BEST TEAM WIN.'
The university team sent a reply saying: 'MAY THE *BETTER* TEAM WIN. WHERE'S YOUR GRAMMAR?'
The secretary sent another wire back: 'PASSED AWAY LAST WEEK. OTHERWISE SHE'D CLIP YOUR EARS FOR BLOODY CHEEK.'

Late night phone call from one of Henpecked Cecil's mates: 'Mrs Cecil? Just phoning to tell you that Cecil was held up as he left the pub.'
'Mugged?'
'No. Drunk.'

The angling team fished a match against a team from the local jail.
'Ah,' said the vicar to the home captain, 'I suppose fishing against your chaps is part of their recreation and rehabilitation.'
'No,' said the captain. 'Fishing against our lot is part of their punishment.'

Jack and Jill went after brill.
Spent all day by the water.
Good job Jill was on the pill.
Brill weren't what Jack was after.

'How many fish have you caught today?'
'When I get another, that'll make one.'

Mary slapped her angler swain.
'What are you, Charlie – kinky?'
'No, you're sitting on my maggots,' he said.
'And I'm looking for a pinkie.'

The angling club from Salford went on a boozy coach trip to Blackpool. No fishing. Just drink all the way, then a crawl round the pubs and clubs till midnight.
The lads staggered back to the coach park and found old Fred spark out on the tarmac.
'He must have left the boozer early,' said his mates. 'Had enough, too, by the look of him. Let's get him home.'
They lifted him into the coach and were all ferried back to Salford. When they arrived, Fred was still unconscious. Two of his mates carried him round to his house and knocked on the door. No reply.
They tried shouting through the letter box to his wife, and eventually threw stones at the window. Still no reply.
The bedroom window of the house opposite was flung open and a neighbour stuck his head out.
'No use trying to raise Fred or his wife,' the neighbour said. 'They're on a fortnight's holiday in Blackpool . . .'

As any married man will tell you, the most difficult thing about fishing is getting out of the house to do it.

'Jackson,' said the boss. 'You took the afternoon off yesterday for an appointment with your dentist. But I saw you on the river bank, fishing with a little fat man in spectacles.'
'That's right, sir. The little fat man in spectacles *is* my dentist.'

'Who's that at the door?'
'A fisherman.'
'Tell him to drop me a line.'

'I was shipwrecked once on a fishing trip and I had to live for a whole week on a tin of sardines.'
'By heck. You were lucky not to fall off.'

Magistrate: 'Did you warn the defendant that he must leave the towpath?'
Irish bailiff: 'Indade Oi did, sorr. Oi said to him, "If yer afther sittin' there yer'll have to move".'
Magistrate: 'What happened then?'
Irish bailiff: 'The defendant rose to his feet, but still didn't move. So Oi told him, "If everbody just stood there loike you're doing, shure nobody would be able to get past".'

Did you hear about the Jewish match captain who opened the peg draw with the toss of a Cohen?

Confucius he say,
Angler on look out
Beat bailiff with book out.

The match team captain gave his anglers a real dressing down.
'Useless, you lot!' he said. 'Couldn't catch a cold in a blizzard! Come down to the canal with me and I'll really show you something.'
The crestfallen team trooped down to the canal, and there the captain tackled up and cast out. After an hour and a half he had snagged his line in the trees, lost several hooks on underwater obstructions, had an argument with a passing bargee, fallen in the water, missed the only two bites he'd had, and not caught a single fish.
'See?' he said. 'That's how you lot have been fishing. And from now on I want to see a drastic improvement!'

'I see you're fishing for the club this afternoon.'
'Yes. But how did you know?'
'The flag on the clubhouse is at half mast.'

Dopy Alec fell overboard from the boat and was attacked by a shark.
'Quick!' he screamed. 'Throw me a knife!'
One of his mates threw a razor-sharp switchblade.
'That's no flaming use!' shouted Alec, throwing it back. 'Haven't you got a fish knife?'

'Do you know how long pike should be played?'
'The same way as short 'uns.'

'Sure you'll be able to get to the club stag do tonight, Cecil?'
'Oh yes. No bother,' said Henpecked Cecil.
'What about the wife? Will she let you out?'
'She'll have a job to stop me,' said Cecil. 'Tonight's the night for her mud beauty treatment. She soaks her feet in a bowlful of mud and puts a mudpack on her face.'
'So?'
'So I've mixed some quick-drying cement with the mud.'

Paddy looked in his tin of maggots.
'Rafferty,' he said, 'some of dese is pointin' de wrong way fer me ter put der hook in.'
'Course dey are,' said Rafferty. 'Dose are fer fishin' on de udder soide.'

The two rival fishing teams had been promised a bottle of beer by their supporters' clubs for each pound of fish caught in the needle match. They made local match history with final weights of 3,754 lbs to 3,693 lbs.

Did you hear about the weight-lifting sea angler who became mussel-bound?

'Dad, what has lots of hairy legs, red and yellow stripes, claws like a lobster, a sting on the end of its tail and lives in water?'
'I don't know, son. Why?'
'Because one's just crawled up the bank and gone right up your trouser leg.'

'Fred fishes a good match, doesn't he?'
'Yes – if you watch him.'

'It was our wedding anniversary,' said Henpecked Cecil. 'And I forgot and went fishing.'
'Catch anything?'
'Not until I got home.'

The angler arrived late at the fishing club social evening and missed the raffle, so he asked the results of it.
'Oh,' said the club chairman, 'I won the first prize. Wasn't I lucky?'
'You were,' said the angler. 'And the second?'
'My wife won the second prize. Wasn't she lucky?'
'She was indeed,' said the angler. 'And the third?'
'Ah, yes. My daughter won the third prize. Wasn't she lucky? By the way, I've just remembered, you haven't paid me for your tickets, yet.'
'So I haven't,' said the angler. 'Aren't I lucky?'

Two old mates, both as deaf as posts, met in the road.
One carried a rod and line.
'Going fishing?' said the other.
'No, I'm going fishing.'
'Oh, I thought from the look of that rod you were going fishing.'
'No. Just a spot of fishing.'
'Pity that. It's a lovely day for fishing.'

Our match team captain won't let his anglers be vaccinated – just in case they don't catch anything.

Confucius he say,
Man with gozzer in pocket
Tickled pinkie all day.

The night fisherman was nearly at the river when it started raining heavily. He ran all the way back home and shouted up to the bedroom window, 'Throw down my waterproof anorak, will you, love?'
The window opened and his nightie-clad wife threw down an anorak.
The angler put it on and started back. Under a street lamp he glanced down at the big badge on the sleeve – and realized he belonged to a club in the next town.

Five members of the bottom-of-the-league fishing club met regularly after every home match to drown their sorrows in the local pub.
By closing time they would all be completely incapable, but the landlord would ring for a taxi, pile them all in, and give the driver his instructions.
'The bloke on the right lives in Stanley Grove, the next one in Mitton Street, and the one on the left in Philip Street. The two sitting opposite them on the fold-down seats both live in Eskdale Avenue.'
This time the taxi drove off down the road, but within five minutes it was back at the pub. The driver jumped out and yelled through the pub letter box, 'Sorry, landlord, could you come and sort these blokes out again? I hit a bump turning the corner.'

Young Jimmy, who'd gone fishing with his father, came home first. And in tears.
'What's the matter?' said his mother.
'Dad caught this huge fish,' said Jimmy. 'And it kept towing him up and down the river bank. All of a sudden his foot slipped and he fell in.'
'Silly boy,' said his mother. 'You shouldn't have cried at a thing like that. You should have laughed.'
'I did.'

'How often do people get drowned on this coast?' asked the nervous shore angler.
'Once is usually enough,' said the old hand.

The Irishman was fishing in the evening with a mate when the most terrible storm sprang up. Thunder, lightning, rain, hail – the lot.
'Hey, Paddy,' said his mate. 'You can't go home in this. Look, I don't live far from the river. Why not come home and spend the night at my place?'
'Most koind of yer,' said Paddy. 'Oi'll just nip home and get me pyjamas.'

The angler rushed into the tackle shop and said, 'A spinner, please – and quick! I've got to catch a bus.'
'Sorry, sir,' said the assistant. 'We don't sell spinners that big.'

Two Irishmen each caught a fish at the same time.
'How will we tell them apart when we take them out of the keepnet?' said Paddy.
'I know,' said Michael. 'We'll put a nick in the tail of one, then we'll be able to tell.'
By mistake, each put a nick in the tail of his own fish.
'Bejasus,' said Paddy, 'We'll never tell them apart now.'
'I've got it,' said Michael. 'You take the pike and I'll take the gudgeon.'

Angling is the simplest of sports. All it needs is a line with a worm on one end and a lunatic on the other.

They asked Albert to act as a steward at the next fishing match.
'I'm not qualified,' he said. 'My parents were married.'

'I had to give up fishing last season,' said Henpecked Cecil, 'for health reasons.'
'Were you catching cold sitting on the bank?'
'No. The wife threatened to kill me.'

A young lady got into a train compartment, the only other occupant of which was a particularly ugly, evil-smelling angler.
The train had only just started off when the angler began, 'Excuse me, love, but . . . '
'Don't you dare start anything,' said the young lady, 'or I'll pull the communication cord!'
'No, but . . . All I want to say is . . . '
'Keep away from me, you horrible, smelly thing! I've told you – one more move and I pull this cord!'
'Yes, but . . . ' said the angler, and started moving closer.
The girl screamed, pulled the cord, and the train screeched to a halt. The guard and the driver both burst into the carriage and demanded to know what was going on.
'He . . . He . . . ' panted the girl.
'He's trying to get that paper bag full of maggots,' said the angler, 'that the young lady's been sitting on for the last quarter of an hour . . . '

'What's the hardest thing to learn about fishing?'
'Getting up at four in the morning.'

An incautious young angler from Consett
Suffered one night from the onset
Of frostbitten toes
And Nightfisher's Nose
'Cos his clogs were being mended, his nose cosy was at the cleaners, and of each he only had one set.

The angler was lurching home after an evening spent drowning his sorrows in the pub.
Halfway across a field, he bumped into a scarecrow with its arms outstretched.
'Lying hound!' he said, taking a couple of steps back so he could focus. 'I told you back in the boozer that you'd never caught a trout that size. So don't come chasing after me now with the same cock-and-bull story . . .'

'By heck, that was rough,' said the fish, flopping back into the river.
'What was the matter?' said his mate. 'Most of the anglers round here are pretty decent. They just take the hook out and throw you back.'
'Yes,' said the roach. 'But this one was a small arms instructor in the army. Specializes in grenades. When he caught me he pulled the hook out, counted to five and lobbed me right over the bridge.'

A man approached the angler on the bank and asked, 'Any luck?'
'Nothing today,' said the angler. 'But yesterday I couldn't go wrong. Caught forty five massive fish from this very spot.'
'Really?' said the stranger. 'Do you know who I am?'
'No.'
'I'm the local magistrate, chairman of the Water Authority, and just happen to own this stretch of private water.'
'Oh, dear,' said the fisherman. 'Do you know who I am?'
'No.'
'The biggest bloody liar for miles.'

After a strenuous night's fishing, the angler got home at dawn. There was still time for a couple of hours' sleep, so he crept into the marital bedroom and got undressed.
'Just a minute!' came his wife's voice from the bed. 'Where's your underwear?'
'My God!' he said. 'I've been robbed!'

Most fairy stories begin with the words, 'Once upon a time . . . ' Others begin with the words, 'There was this fish, and it must have been all of four feet long . . . '

The prize for boasting went to the angler who strained himself in the pub trying to show the size of the bait.

Mary married a coarse fisherman,
And on their honeymoon
Said, 'What are you thinking of now, my love?'
'Tench,' he said. 'It's June.'

The angler on a deep sea boat trip had been pestered all morning by an American tourist who was fishing next to him.

Nothing British angling could offer, said the American, was a patch on things in the States.

'Why, I've caught tuna fish that needed a crane to winch them on deck,' said the American. 'Bluefins that leapt so high out of the water it took them ten minutes to come down. Shark so powerful that they dragged the boat miles off course. And once I caught a fish so big that the others wouldn't let me haul it into the boat in case it capsized.'

'I know just how you feel,' said the Englishman.

'It happened to me once – aboard the QE2.'

The American went on boasting until eventually the English angler got stuck into a 400-lb Mako shark. The battle raged for an hour until finally the monster was winched on deck and lay there thrashing and snapping.

'Gee,' said the American. 'Not bad. Not bad at all. What were you using for bait?'

'*That*,' said the Englishman, pointing to the shark. 'I was just reeling in to see if it was all right.'

Confucius he say,
Fishing with wind in face better than
fishing with frostbite in long johns.

The class had no interest at all in English essay writing. All the boys could talk about was fishing. So one day the English master had the bright idea of asking them to describe a fishing match in an essay.

Most of them did very well, writing at length on the subject dearest to their hearts. But young Sid was not going to be caught like that. His essay consisted of just two words:

'No Contest'.

The fishing team had a girl mascot who was so thin that when she swallowed a grape six anglers joined the army. Mind you, she'd always said she was too good to give herself to any one man. That's why she shared herself out among the whole team.

'I've dated every member of the match team, and I haven't made love to one of them,' she confided to her friend.

'Don't tell me,' said her friend. 'I bet it's that bald-headed, knock-kneed one with the specs . . .' →

A CAUTIONARY RHYME FOR ANGLERS:

Old Fred Cole was a crafty old soul
And a match secretary was he.
He lined up his team,
Said, 'We're going for bream',
And called for his fiddlers three.

Eeny, Meeny, Miny were the fiddlers.
Pity there weren't no Mo.
But Mo had been banned the last time out,
So today he couldn't go.

They fished all morn till well past noon,
Till their arms felt just like jelly.
Then each jolly fiddler made up his catch
With kippers kept down each welly.

'What's this, what's this, what's this?'
Said the steward man.
'A sordid bid for wealth?'
'Goes to prove,' said the fiddlers,
Weighing kippers with the tiddlers,
'That smoking can damage your health.'

Though Old Fred Cole was a crafty old soul
And a match secretary was he,
He's now stuck away in jail
Sewing bags up for the mail,
And so are his fiddlers three . . .

A COUPLE OF PAGES OF FIBS

. . . Just to keep you in practice

'This fish I've caught,' said Jim, 'weighs 25lb if it's an ounce.'
'Give over,' said his mate. 'I've got my scales here. Let's try it.'
The fish weighed in at 4½lb.
'Would you believe it?' said Jim. 'The bloody thing's hollow!'

Not all fishermen are born liars. Some are born honest. But they have to learn to get over it.

The American on the boat was boasting again.
'I caught a shark,' he said, 'that measured forty two feet from its nose to its tail.'
'I caught a skate,' said the Englishman, 'which was so vast it could only be measured in acres. One and a half acres, that skate covered.'
'Just a minute, buddy,' said the American. 'I don't think you're telling the whole truth there.'
'Tell you what,' said the Englishman. 'Knock ten feet off that shark and I'll have another look at my skate.'

'All I caught on my last trip out was just one fish. One measly fish.'
'And what did you do with it?'
'I got a couple of fellers to help me throw it back.'

The angler was sitting alone in the pub, talking to himself. After a while it got quite noisy.
'Excuse me,' said the barman, 'but there's only you in here. What are you getting so heated about?'
'I caught a fish today,' said the angler. 'A whole fish. There's nobody else here to tell the story to, so I'm lying to myself about the weight.'

'So you want to join our fishing club. Do you tell lies?'
'No. But I can soon learn.'

'If that fish you caught was as long as you reckon, how the hell did you get it home?'
'Easy. It was a corridor train.'

The only fisherman who could claim that a lie never passed his lips was the one who talked down his nose.

An Indian angler named Moti
Felt some teeth closing over his dhoti.
He said, 'Oh, dear me.
'It's a big manatee.
'And they're only supposed to eat loti.'

Henpecked Cecil was in trouble.
'You're going fishing *again*?' yelled his wife.
'If you were to spend just one weekend at home I'd die of shock!'
'Steady on, love,' said Cecil. 'You know I don't take bribes.'

Landladies who advertise fishing holidays always have special terms for anglers: Cash In Advance.

The old laird wanted his rather dim son to do well on the ancestral salmon beat. So he bought him the finest rod and tackle money could buy, and sent him down to the river with the estate's oldest, most experienced and most trusted ghillie. At the end of the day the boy and the ghillie returned, and the laird called the ghillie into his presence.
'Tell me now, Angus,' he said, 'and with no prevarication. How did the boy do out on the river today?'
'Marvellously, m'laird. Supairbly,' said Angus. 'If I may be pairmitted tae say so, even magnificently. But today Providence saw fit tae be mairciful tae the fish.'

A mate met Henpecked Cecil on the bank.
'Hey,' he said. 'Was that your wife who was fishing with you last week?'
'Damn silly question that is,' said Cecil. 'Would I have a girlfriend that ugly?'

The angler on a fishing holiday in Ireland was a bit apprehensive as Seamus steered the boat through some rough water on the river.
'Don't worry, sorr, at all at all,' shouted Seamus. 'Oi know every rock in this river, so Oi do.'
Just then there was a sickening crunch. A jagged rock appeared through the bottom of the boat and torrents of water poured in.
'Didn't Oi tell yer, sorr?' shouted Seamus. 'Oi know every rock on this river. And that there is one of the big ones . . .'

The angler had been complaining to the vicar about the state of the fishing, the amount of weed on the water, the terrible weather . . . just about everything.
'It's all part of God's plan,' said the vicar. 'We have much to be thankful for. Even the humble fish are fed every day.'
'Yes,' said the angler. 'With my flaming groundbait.'

Bailiff: This young lady angler had a forged season ticket for the water.'
Magistrate: 'Counterfeit?'
Bailiff: 'Yes, your worship. She had two.'

Mary seduced a match steward,
And said, 'How was it? Great?'
'You're disqualified, my love,' he said,
'For using illegal bait.'

There had been a midnight robbery at the trout farm. Thousands of young trout had been netted and carried off, possibly to be sold as stock fish to an unsuspecting angling club.

Down came a detective from Scotland Yard. Unerringly, with his 'tec's instinct, he went for the local poacher, took the old boy out to the pub, bought him a beer, and then got round to the subject of the robbery.

'Oh, arr,' said the old poacher. 'Oi knows 'oo 'ad they trout all roight . . .'

'Really?' said the detective, feigning indifference. 'Have another pint.'

'Thank 'ee koindly. *Shlurrp* . . . What was we talkin' about?'

'Another pint?' said the detective.

'Very civil of 'ee. *Shlurrp* . . . Oh, arrr . . . They trout. Oi knows 'oo 'ad 'em all roight. But sometoimes me old memory . . .'

'Another pint?'

'Wouldn't say no. *Shlurrp* . . . Yer . . . As Oi were sayin' . . . Feller 'oo 'ad them trout were Cap'n Tintwhistle 'oo owns the trout farm. But 'ee ain't got 'em now . . .'

A scientist invented a hair restorer that would grow hair on a lobworm. It made his fortune, but it ruined his fishing.

A goose-pimpled angler from Tottenham
Cried, 'Oh dearie me – I've forgotten 'em!
'I've started to sneeze
'And without 'em I'll freeze.
'What's warm I can put my cold bottom on?'

Joe was boasting to a neighbour about the big pike he'd caught the day before.
'Massive, it was. Head like the front of a tank. Teeth that would take your arm off. Nearly as much as I could do to lift it.'
'Amazing,' said the neighbour. 'And where is it now?'
'Daddy was ever so kind,' piped up Joe's little daughter. 'When he got home last night he cooked it and gave it to the cat.'

This great monster octopus crawled out of the sea, up the beach, and into a pub on the front.
'Pint of bitter, please landlord,' it said.
'Certainly, sir. That'll be 75p.'
The octopus paid up, drank his pint, and turned to go.
'Excuse me, sir,' said the landlord. 'I know this is a fisherman's pub and all that, and don't think I'm being personal, but we don't get many monster octopuses in here.'
'With bitter at 75p a pint,' said the octopus, 'I'm not bloody surprised.'

The main charm of mixed night fishing is that the excitement is in tents.

Confucius he say,
Man with spinner up nose
Dink id dot berry fuddy.

Dopy Alec went shark fishing. When the boat came back he was rushed straight to hospital.

'What happened?' asked a man on the quayside.

'Alec caught a shark,' explained his mate. 'And instead of gaffing it to bring it in, he stuck his arm right down its throat. By gum, they won't call him Dopy any more after this.'

'What will they call him?'

'Lefty.'

To ensure fairness in the peg draw, the match officials agreed to ask the first person they met on the street to perform the task. They found an old gentleman who not only agreed, but who offered them the use of his new hat from which to make the draw.

All the screwed-up bits of paper were placed in the hat. The old boy reached in, pulled out a bit of paper and peered at it short-sightedly.

'Six and seven-eighths,' he announced.

'And who said you could fish here?' asked the bailiff.

'Lord Tomnoddy,' said the angler.

'This is Lord Dolittle's water,' said the bailiff. 'Lord Tomnoddy's water is half a mile upstream.'

'In that case,' said the angler, 'I'll just reel in and wait till it gets here.'

'That fishing holiday you had was really cheap. Were the digs OK for that money?'
'Fine. Just one snag, though. I kept getting disturbed in the morning.'
'How come?'
'Well, at six o'clock the chambermaid got up to do the cleaning and woke me up. At half past six the landlady got up to make the breakfast and woke me up. At seven o'clock her husband got up for work and woke me up. Then, one by one, the landlady's four kids got up, and they woke me up. By half past eight, though, it was fairly quiet.'
'Nobody else to get up?'
'No. And I had the bed all to myself.'

The expert from the Fisheries Department visited the trout farm.
'I'm here to tell you,' he said to the farmer, 'that different diets will have different effects on the fish.'
'That explains it,' said the farmer, who wasn't as daft as he looked. 'I fed the fish one year on sawdust. Half of 'em grew up with wooden legs and the other half were woodpeckers.'

The visitor to the lunatic asylum saw an inmate dangling a line from a rod into a bucket of water.
'And what are we doing here?' he said, ingratiatingly. 'Fishing, are we?'
'Fishing?' said the loony. 'In a bucket? And they keep trying to tell me *I'm* barmy!'

SONGS FOR SWINGING CONGER FISHERMEN:
Eel Meet Again.
Tie Me Conger Eel Down, Sport.
Congeratulations.
Eel, Aye, Addio, You've Won The Cup.
Aye, Aye, Conger.
Teeth For Two.
Fangs For The Memory.

Two anglers were wading in the surf in Australia, when along came a pack of man-eating sharks.
'Help!' cried one of the anglers. 'A shark has bitten my leg off!'
'Which one?'
'How the hell should I know? They all look alike to me!'

Bailiff: 'I'm nabbing you for poaching. Name?'
Angler: 'Oliphant Marmaduke Gascoigne D'Arcy Peregrine Chuckerbutty.'
Bailiff: (putting notebook away): 'All right, then. Just don't let it happen again.'

'I'm fed up with the way you treat my daughter,' said the angler's mother-in-law. 'Always going off fishing and leaving her alone. When you're dead and gone, I'll dance on your grave.'
So the angler arranged to be buried at sea.

Two mates went out fishing and afterwards finished off the day in the pub. One angler came back alone. When he got home he burst into tears.

'What's up, love?' said his wife. 'And where's Jimmy?'

'Dead,' he sobbed. 'Drowned.'

'How terrible! What happened?'

'On the way back from the pub he tried to jump the canal. In two jumps!'

What do you call a 6ft. 6in., 18-stone bailiff?

Sir.

A specimen hunter from Wigan
Cried, 'Hey up – I'm into a big 'un!'
He didn't half hoot
When out came a boot
And a tree with a solitary twig on.

The club duffer somehow wangled his way into the match team. From the first whistle he did everything wrong: scared the fish, tangled his tackle, cast into other anglers' swims. You name it, he did it.

'Hey, Arnold!' shouted the bloke sitting at the next peg. 'Isn't this a bit dangerous for somebody like you?'

'What do you mean?' said Arnold. 'I'm doing all right. And how could I come to any harm out here?'

'Well, I'd put your cap on for a start,' shouted the other angler. 'There's a woodpecker about.'

BAILIF

'Do you like codling?'
'I don't know. I've never coddled.'

'How did old Jim make a mess of his right hand like that?'
'Shark fishing. He put his hand in a shark's mouth to see how many teeth it had.'
'And what happened?'
'The shark closed its mouth to see how many fingers Jim had.'

Henpecked Cecil was in trouble with his wife. He'd forgotten their wedding anniversary, and she was in tears at the breakfast table.
'I bet you don't remember one single thing about our wedding day,' she sniffed.
'I do, I do,' he said. 'The wedding was in the afternoon. That gave me the chance to nip down to the river in the morning, and I caught that beautiful 25lb. pike.'

'How did the fishing match go?'
'Lousy. They beat us with an aggregate of 715 lb. to nothing.'
'To nothing?'
'Yes. And we were damn lucky to get that.'

He's what you might call an original angler.
He makes lots of mistakes but they're different every time.

Confucius he say,
Chippy better for dinner
Than banking on spinner.

Before he went out sea fishing in a hired motor boat, Fred had learned all the necessary signals for survival. Down came a thick fog and he headed back for land. Suddenly a tall shape loomed up in front of him. A light kept flashing on and off, and Fred could just make out the form of a man leaning over a rail.
Fred skimmed quickly through his signal manual, but could make no sense of what he was confronted with. So he shouted across, 'Belay there! What are you trying to do – scuttle yourself?'
The man at the rail shouted back, 'I'd have a bloody job – this is a lighthouse!'

They play the National Anthem after our home fishing matches just to see if the team can stand up.

Heard about the Irishman who couldn't get the hang of tickling a trout?
He could never locate its armpits.

'I hear the angling club is looking for a new treasurer.'
'That's right.'
'But I thought they appointed a new treasurer only last month?'
'That's the one they're looking for.'

Dopy Alec was finally expelled from the match team, and his removal was being discussed by a club member and the team captain.
'Shame, really,' said the member. 'Alec was a nice enough chap. How long was he with you?'
'That was the trouble,' said the captain. 'He was never with us – always against us.'

Two poachers were waiting for the bailiff on his rounds so that they could give him a good clobbering.
Half an hour past the expected time the bailiff had not put in an appearance.
'Hey,' said one of the poachers, 'I hope nothing's happened to the poor feller.'

The vicar stopped a small boy on the river bank on a Sunday morning.
'Do you know where little boys go who fish on the Sabbath?' he asked, sternly.
'Yes, vicar. Generally to that run under the trees over there. But if it's been raining . . .'

Mary caught a great big eel,
Six feet long, or longer.
She's as well as can be expected now
After trying to dance the conger.

An angler broke his arm and had to have it put in plaster. When the plaster was set he said, 'Doctor, when you take this off will I be able to win first prize in the fly casting championships?'
'Of course you will,' said the doctor.
'Hey, that's good,' said the angler. 'I never could before.'

The novice angler entered the casting competition and got a bit flustered towards the end because the judge kept walking around him looking at a dial in the palm of his hand.
'Look,' said the angler. 'I'm getting a bit fed up with this. This isn't a timed competition, you know, so just stop looking at your watch!'
'This isn't a watch,' said the judge. 'It's a compass.'

During a hard fought fishing match, lots of insults were being shouted at the individual anglers, but one woman kept shouting, 'Kill the steward! Kill the steward!'
'Who's that?' whispered one of the anglers.
'It's his wife,' came the reply.

'Refresh my memory,' said the drunken angler to his mate in the pub. 'What weight did our team catch this afternoon?'
'Four pounds, three ounces.'
'And what weight did the opposition get?'
'Two hundred and twelve pounds, six ounces.'
'Refresh my memory again. Who won?'

'I can understand your annoyance at being beaten in the fishing match by what you considered unfair means,' said the magistrate. 'But you *were* drunk, you *did* start a fight, and it *did* take six policemen to put you in a cell last night. Have you anything to say in mitigation?'
The little angler in the dock said, 'Yes, your worship. It only took one of 'em to let me out this morning.'

'I didn't see you in church this morning, Fred, and I'm told you went to the charity football match instead.'
'That's not true, vicar – and I've got the fish to prove it.'

'Dopy Alec was fishing in that private lake the other day.'
'Did he get anything?'
'Yes. Prosecuted.'

An incautious young angler from Delhi
Had a damp feeling inside his welly.
    The waters of the Ganges
    Rose over his phalanges.
He should have stayed home with the telly.

The old angler went to see his pal, who was dying.

'Don't worry, love,' he said to the sorrowing wife. 'I'll cheer him up. And if he's got something to look forward to, he could even make a miraculous recovery.'

So he went into the bedroom where his old friend lay, looking absolutely ghastly.

'Hello, me old son,' he said chirpily. 'My, my, you're looking a ton better today. Listen – your missis is coming up with some nourishing soup and some chicken sandwiches. We've got to get your strength up because your name's been put down for the "A" team in next week's match. They reckon there's only you good enough to pull in the weights we need against the opposition.'

The angler sat up, hope and interest in his eyes, drank the soup and ate the sandwiches. And all the time his mate was chatting on about the match and the team's certainty of winning so long as their star angler was recovered enough to fish.

At the end of half an hour, all traces of illness had vanished, and the invalid was talking animatedly about the baits and methods he intended to use.

Suddenly his mate noticed the time. 'Excuse me, old lad,' he said. 'I've got to go. Match committee meeting at three. I'll tell 'em you'll be there on the day.'

On the way out he banged his head on a low beam in the bedroom.

'Bloody 'ell,' he said. 'They'll never get your coffin through there.'

This is the one they swear is true:
An angler, boat fishing, was taken suddenly seasick and lost his false teeth overboard.
For a joke, his mate took out his own false teeth, tied them to his line, and pretended to catch them.
'Here you are, Jim,' he said. 'How's that for a million-to-one chance? I've hooked your false teeth.'
Jim took the false teeth, put them in his mouth and found they didn't fit.
'Sorry, Harry,' he said. 'These aren't mine at all,' – and threw them overboard.

Somebody came looking for Henpecked Cecil.
'Is your husband in?' he asked Mrs Cecil.
'No, he's not!' she snapped. 'He's out fishing again.'
'This is rather urgent. Can you tell me where he is and how I can recognize him?'
'Easy,' said Mrs Cecil. 'Just go down to the river bank and look for a rod with a worm on each end.'

'I understand you're not fishing for our club team this week.'
'Certainly not. Not after what the captain said to me after the last match.'
'What was that?'
'You're through.'

Confucius he say,
Angler who win
Get filled up with gin;
Angler who lose
Buy his own booze.

The frogman was exploring the bottom of a very deep lake, and was using really sophisticated diving gear to combat the water pressure and other hazards of such a depth.
Suddenly he saw another man, fully dressed and clutching a fishing rod, descending through the murky water. The frogman was amazed. He wrote on his underwater message pad: 'What the hell are you doing down here?'
The angler grabbed the pad and pencil and wrote back: 'Drowning, you fool!'

Young Randy, out night fishing with his girlfriend, was interrupted when a bailiff tripped over one of the tent ropes.
'Hey, you two in there!' shouted the bailiff. 'Don't you think you'd be better off in bed?'
'Too right we would,' said Randy. 'But we're not doing too badly in here.'

Bailiff: 'I know you. You've got 20 previous convictions for poaching.'
Angler: 'Well, nobody's perfect.'

'Waiter! Are you sure that's real salmon mousse?'
'Of course, sir. Why do you ask?'
'I just bent over to sniff it and two fistfuls of fish fingers grabbed me by the throat.'

'Good fishing trip?'
'I'll say. We got £75 back on the empties.'

The match team was fishing in Holland, but when the plane was due to take off from Heathrow, six of the team were missing, presumed drunk. Just then, up to the plane screeched a little red refuelling truck. Clinging to the back of it were three of the missing anglers. They leapt off and scrambled aboard the plane.
The plane flew across to Holland, landed at Schipol Airport, and another red refuelling truck whizzed across the tarmac.
'Don't worry, captain,' said one of the first drunken three. 'The other lads are bound to have caught this next truck. By gum, though, it must have shifted to get here by this time . . .'

'These trout you've cooked, my love,' said Henpecked Cecil, 'are a bit off. I don't think you cooked them soon enough.'
'Correction,' said Mrs Cecil. 'You didn't catch them soon enough.'

The middle-aged man walked into the large firm and asked to see the manager.
'My name is Parker,' he said. 'My nephew, Eric, works here as an office boy and I promised to take him fishing today. I've called to ask if you would let him have the afternoon off.'
'I'd be only too happy to oblige,' said the manager. 'But for the fact that he's already been given the afternoon off to go to your funeral.'

'Does a fishing team have positions like a soccer team?' asked Dopy Alec.
'No,' said his mate. 'Why?'
'Well, I just heard our captain telling somebody that I was the team's main drawback.'

The angler rang the doctor and said, 'My little boy has just swallowed my porcupine quill float. I'll bring him round in the morning.'
'In the morning?' said the doctor. 'This could be serious. What are you going to do till then?'
'Oh, it's all right, doctor. I'll use one of my cane floats.'

The fish is the only creature on earth that takes its holidays at the same time as the angler.

The best week of the year for catching fish is always last week, when they were biting.

An enterprising tackle dealer with a shop near the local lunatic asylum chatted up the psychiatrist in charge one day.

'Look,' he said. 'Why don't you encourage your patients to take up fishing? It's very soothing, very therapeutic. Make the world of difference to their well being. You've got a big lake in the grounds, anyway, and I'll be happy to sell them all the tackle they want.'

'Good idea,' said the psychiatrist. 'Just one thing, though. We can't trust the poor lads with money. They don't know the value of it. So if they offer to pay in milk tops, just accept them and I'll settle up with you at the end of the month.'

'You're on,' said the tackle dealer.

Every weekday for a month the shop was packed with patients from the asylum. They bought so much tackle and bait that the dealer was constantly phoning the wholesalers to order fresh supplies.

At the end of the month, in came the psychiatrist.

'How did you get on with my lads?' he asked.

'Marvellous,' said the dealer. 'No trouble at all. They bought no end of stuff and paid for it all, just as you said, in milk bottle tops.'

'Great,' said the psychiatrist. 'Well, I'd better settle up with you now. What's the damage?'

'Five thousand seven hundred and forty three pounds 11½p, including VAT,' said the dealer.

'Seems reasonable to me,' said the psychiatrist. 'Can you give me change for this manhole cover?'

A match fisherman from Devizes
Ran away with all of the prizes.
    There was just one small snag;
    They fell out of the bag,
And now he's awaiting Assizes.

Young Jimmy was showing his schoolfriend the family holiday snaps. One was of his father holding a hideous looking angler fish.
'Just look,' said Jimmy, 'at that horrible great ugly thing.'
'Yes,' said his pal. 'But what's that he's holding?'

'Don't know what the world's coming to,' moaned the old Scottish angler. 'Everywhere you go on the river bank there are rowdies making the most awful din. If it's not their motorbikes it's their transistor radios. It got so bad the other week I could hardly hear myself practising the bagpipes.'

A man walked into a pet shop and said, 'Have you got any goldfish going cheap?'
'Got some canaries like that, sir,' said the assistant. 'But the goldfish just go *bloop . . . bloop . . .*'

Old Jim never fished a match without his lucky rabbit's foot. And it worked. The only match this year in which he never caught anything was the last one. He missed it because he lost his lucky charm. He'd dropped it in the road and went back to get it. Pity he didn't see the bus . . .

These days the basic necessity of fishing costs about four times as much as it used to. And most of it isn't fit to drink.

Confucius he say
Pike down trousers
Better than piranha in bath.
But probably not much.

The two Irish lads were out fishing in a boat when the vessel sprang a massive leak in the bows.
Mick knocked a big hole in the hull at the stern.
'That's all roight now, Liam,' he said. 'This'll let it out, so it will.'

Bailiff: 'Are you a poacher?'
Eighteen-stone bruiser: 'Yes. What of it?'
Bailiff: 'Lucky for you I've just finished for the day.'

The angler climbed into the railway carriage, soaking wet, covered in mud and slime, smelling of beer, laden with gear and starting to steam: the usual condition of an angler after a hard day's fishing.
He was met with very stern stares and much curling of the lip from a very haughty lady sitting opposite.
'Don't let it worry yer, love,' he said. 'We lost the match today. And I'm committing suicide at the first tunnel . . .'

'Do you like pouting?'
'Can't remember – it's so long since I've pouted.'

The applicant for the bailiff's job was asked as part of the general knowledge test: 'How long is the River Amazon?'
'I don't know,' he said. 'But if that's going to be my beat, you can stick the job!'

Dopy Alec was walking home from the river with a huge pike under his arm.
'Hello,' said his mate. 'Nice fish, that. Are you taking him home for dinner?'
'No, he's had his dinner,' said Alec. 'I did think of taking him to the pictures.'

'Hey! When you cast out then you nearly hit my wife with that heavy lead!'
'Sorry. Want me to try again?'

The hypochondriac angler who was hoping for a doctor's certificate for a few days off work, complained that he was suffering from a rare type of disease brought about by strain and over-exertion.
'Ridiculous,' said the doctor. 'You'd never know if you had that disease. It's one of the most difficult in the world to diagnose: there are no outward signs, no aches or pains – in fact there's no way you could tell there was anything wrong with you.'
'That's it,' said the angler. 'My symptoms exactly.'

The Irishman went back to the tackle shop.
'These waders you sold me are too short,' he said. 'The water came right over the top.'
'I think you'll find, sir,' said the assistant, 'that the waders are not short at all. It's the river that's too tall.'
'And why should the river be taller than me?'
'It's probably older, sir.'
'Yer know, I never thought of that. Bejasus, them ducks must be bobbin' on a bit.'

Confucius he say,
Squid bait up nose
Not smell much like rose.

The lady angler, fishing in a state of advanced pregnancy, was suddenly taken ill on the bank.
When the ambulance turned up, there were cries of 'Hot water! Hot water!' from somewhere in the crowd.
'Has the baby arrived, then?' shouted an anxious ambulanceman.
'No,' said one of the anglers. 'I'm trying to make a cup of cocoa.'

Back from his holiday, the angler asked for two more weeks off to get married.
'But you've just had a fortnight,' said the boss. 'Couldn't you have got married then?'
'What?' said the angler. 'And ruin my fishing?'

'Can't understand old Arthur drowning himself,' said Henpecked Cecil. 'He wasn't even married.'

There was a young angler from Leeds
Who swallowed a packet of seeds.
His whiskers grew roots
Right down to his boots
And his swingtip was covered in weeds.

Dopy Alec was so stupid that when he caught a brilliantly spotted rainbow trout, he threw it back. He thought it was a brown trout with measles.

Cecil was really henpecked, but now and again he rebelled – usually after an outing with the lads from the fishing club.
One night in the pub, after a particularly happy day out, he was well and truly plastered.
'Careful, Cecil,' said his mate. 'If you go home in that state, your wife will hit the ceiling.'
'I hope so,' giggled Cecil. 'Last time the bullet went right through my ear.'

Talking about epidemics, Alec was so slow that he went fishing once and came back with only one mump.

'I've caught a haddock!'
'A finnan?'
'No – a fick 'un!'

Henpecked Cecil called in at the fishmonger's for his usual brace of trout after failing to catch any himself.
A lady customer who'd just been to the butcher's put her parcel of sausages on the counter while she sorted out some change, and Cecil picked up the wrong packet.
'What do you think of my catch today, my love?' he called from the dining room as his wife was preparing the meal in the kitchen.
'Better than usual,' said Mrs Cecil. 'But there's not a lot left when you've filletted them, is there?'

The shortsighted old professor was taken for his first trip out in Scotland after salmon.
After a particularly energetic cast over to the opposite bank he started reeling in and cried, 'What have I here? A fish of the species *salmo salar*, order *Salmoniformes*? A truly wild fish?'
'No,' said his ghillie. 'A bailiff of the species *homo sapiens*, order *Primates*. Name of Angus MacTavish. And by the look of him he's awfu' wild . . .'

A fish is the only creature on earth that keeps on growing after death.

The heavily laden angler hailed a taxi.
'How much to the river?' he said.
'Two pounds 50 pence, sir,' said the taxi driver.
'And how much for my gear?'
'Fifty pence.'
'Right. Take my gear to the river and I'll follow on.'

The angler was on the dole and fishing for the pot.
He'd not had a single bite, but he did manage to grab a duck which came too close.
He was plucking the duck and putting the feathers in a pile at his feet, when he spied the bailiff approaching.
Quickly he threw the duck into the water.
'And what do you think you're doing?' asked the bailiff.
'I'm minding his clothes while he has a swim,' said the angler.

The captain of the fishing team was surprised to see that among the members of the opposition team was a horse. Not only that, the horse turned out to be the best angler in the team, and contributed a great deal towards its final victory.
'By heck,' said the captain, striding over after the match to shake hands with the opposition and congratulate the horse. 'Well done. How did you learn to fish like that?'
'How does anybody learn?' said the horse. 'Practice, I suppose.'

What's thick and yellow and very dangerous?
Shark-infested custard.

A Scottish pike fisher from Troon
Made a dreadful mistake with a spoon.
It gave quite a tilt
To the front of his kilt
And his sporran just wouldn't lie doon.

A fanatical angler found out that his best friend was having an affair with his wife. So he challenged him to a fishing match to decide who should have her.
'And just to make it interesting, old boy,' he said, 'how about a fiver on the side?'

The unsuccessful angler had been sitting in the bar all night, trying to forget the fish he'd never caught. Every so often his eyes wandered to an enormous pike in a glass case behind the bar. It was the record for the area, caught 30 years earlier, and no fish since had ever matched it.

The angler got more and more morose, more and more drunk. Eventually it was closing time and the landlord said, 'Come on, me old son. I know you've had a trying day, but it *is* time we all went home.'

'Before I go,' said the angler, lurching from his stool, 'I just want to say one thing about that fish over there.'

'And what's that?' said the landlord.

'The man who caught it . . . was a bloody liar!'

A little known social service is Anglers Anonymous. You dial a number and listen to a pack of lies.

EPITAPH FOR AN ANGLER:

Here lies a great angler
And an honest man.
It's not often they bury
Two of 'em together.

An adventurous angler from Bray
Took a slow boat to China one day.
He was pinned to the tiller
By a sex-starved gorilla.
And China's a bloody long way.

The angling club fixed up a match with a team from the local prison.
When the prison team arrived at the bank, the home captain counted them and said, 'Just a minute. We've got 20 men in our team and you've got 35 in yours.'
'So?' said the prison team captain. 'That's what we're inside for – cheating.'

Henpecked Cecil got on the bus. The conductor said, 'Don't tell me – 25p. To the hospital.'
'Yes,' said Cecil. 'How did you know?'
'You've had a row with your wife, haven't you?' said the conductor. 'About your fishing.'
'Yes,' said Cecil. 'I've had a row with my wife. It was about my fishing. And now I'm on the way to hospital. But how did you know all this?'
'Easy,' said the conductor. 'You've still got the rod rest sticking through your head.'

'Are you familiar with Izaak Walton?'
'Familiar! I was fishing with him only yesterday.'
'But he's been dead nearly 300 years.'
'I thought he wasn't saying much.'

Two Red Indians fishing. One of them caught a mermaid.
He carefully took out the hook, looked longingly at the beautiful creature, then threw her back in.
His mate said, 'Why?'
The Redskin said, 'How?'

It was the funeral of the wife of a keen angler. On top of the coffin lay a rod and two cans of bait.
'Here, Charlie,' said the angler's mate. 'I didn't know your dear departed was keen on fishing?'
'She wasn't,' said Charlie. 'But the funeral doesn't end till three. And I've got a match at half past.'

'I say, I say, I say! This fish has no nose.'
'That fish has no nose? How does it smell?'
'Terrible.'

Henpecked Cecil's wife finally died, and he realized that at last he would be free to do as much fishing as he liked.
After the funeral, he collected his rods and went straight down to the river. He had just made his first cast when there was a clap of thunder and a flash of lightning immediately overhead. The lightning hit a tree behind Cecil and blasted off a branch which dropped right on his head.
'By heck,' said Cecil, looking up at the sky, 'it's not taken her long to get up there.'

Fishing: A jerk at one end of a stick waiting for a jerk at the other.

a bit of jostling at the weigh-in, and suddenly e anglers was down on his hands and knees e scales, scuffling about in the mixture of dirt, les, maggot skins and slime.

are you looking for, Harry?' said his mate.

looking for my toffee,' said Harry.

n't be daft. It won't be any use to you anyways if among all that horrible mess.'

's not that,' said Harry. 'My teeth are in it.'

Finally, an old Chinese proverb:
May the tiddler of happiness
Never swim through the hole
In your keepnet.